The Hundreds

The Hundreds

Lauren Berlant &
Kathleen Stewart

DUKE UNIVERSITY PRESS Durham and London 2019

Printed in the United States of America on
acid-free paper ∞
Designed by Amy Ruth Buchanan
Typeset in Huronia and Merope Sans
by Copperline Books

Library of Congress Cataloging-
in-Publication Data
Names: Berlant, Lauren Gail, [date] author. |
Stewart, Kathleen, [date] author.
Title: The hundreds / Lauren Berlant and
Kathleen Stewart.
Description: Durham : Duke University
Press, 2019. | Includes bibliographical
references and indexes.
Identifiers: LCCN 2018026387 (print)
LCCN 2018028497 (ebook)
ISBN 9781478003335 (ebook)
ISBN 9781478001836 (hardcover : alk. paper)
ISBN 9781478002888 (pbk. : alk. paper)
Subjects: LCSH: Authorship—Social
aspects. | Authorship—Political aspects. |
Authorship—Technique. | Creation
(Literary, artistic, etc.)—Social aspects.
Classification: LCC PN145 (ebook) |
LCC PN145 .B474 2019 (print) |
DDC 808.02—dc23
LC record available at
https://lccn.loc.gov/2018026387

Cover art: Laura Heit, *Two Ways Down*,
2015. Animated installation.

Contents

II. INDEXES

Preludic

We are lucky to have collaborators: never taking creative labor for granted, we give unbounded gratitude to Andrew Causey, Susan Lepselter, Fred Moten, and Stephen Muecke, who responded to our request to index the book with shrewd and thoughtful creativity. Indexing is the first interpretation of a book's body. So, rather than presuming the standard taxonomic form—which is its own achievement—we gave the task over to writers whose take on things always surprises us, in part because their style of critical thought generates power in twists of voice and craft. We included blank pages at the end of the book for your own experiments in indexing. We did a little more formal playing in the section "Some Things We Thought With."

Gratitude also for reading, editing, and assembling to Carmen Merport, Ken Wissoker, and the anonymous Duke University Press readers. There were audiences at the University of Chicago, the WTF Affect conference, and the many places where we read solo: thanks for considering the experiment with us. Appreciation to those who gave extensive feedback (for LB, Claudia Rankine, David Simon, Jerry Passannante, Ian Horswill, Keston Sutherland, Carmen Merport; for KS, Jason Pine, Susan Harding, Donna Haraway, Lesley Stern, Ann Cvetkovich, Derek McCormack, Craig Campbell, Joey Russo).

The Austin Public Feelings group was where it all began. It is usual in Public Feelings writing workshops to work with five hundred words on a scene, thing, or situation. Sometimes participants write from a prompt in real time, and others they prepare, but each always reads aloud, the others listening compositionally. In 2012 in Austin, Circe Sturm told us about a one-hundred-word poetics exercise that she'd learned from the estimable Emily Bernard in the context of the "100-Word Collective." Circe took it to ethnographic writing. We brought it to the concept of the new ordinary we'd been developing, and *The Hundreds* project took off. The process has changed our writing, and much else.

The constraint of the book is that our poems (makings) are exercises in following out the impact of things (words, thoughts, people, objects, ideas, worlds) in hundred-word units or units of hundred multiples. Honoring the contingency of the experiment, there is no introduction up front but distributed commentary throughout the book, plus reflection in many spots about how the writing attempts to get at a scene or process a hook. We don't want to say much in advance about what kind of event of reading or encounter the book can become. We tried not to provide even this preliminary.

A hundred words isn't a lot. We made individual hundreds, series of hundreds, and very long hundreds but held to the exact. Some separate pieces became joined and reframed, and the theoretical reflections were shaped as hundreds and folded into the analytic, observational, and transferential ways we move. We wrote through the edit. Every edit set off a cascade of word falls, Rubik's Cubes, tropes, infrastructures, genres, rhymes and off-rhymes, tonal flips and half-steps this way and that. But if the number "hundred" had weather effects it was also tricky: every word-processing program has its own way of determining what a word is before the count goes down. "Word count" might as well be the hastily written notes of a conversation recalled a few hours later. We did the best we could to attain consistency within the constraint of one-hundred-word multiples. If you count more or fewer, you're not coming onto an Easter Egg or a secret door leading to a world for the special people or prisoners but just seeing what the counters we used said we had. (600)

I. The Hundreds

First Things

Every day a friend across the ocean wakes up to suicidal thoughts. Another friend takes a drink to eat clean and another eats a candy bar in bed before washing the sheets, doing laundry naked to ensure soft sleeps. Another friend chants before going out to her analogy lab. Another hires retired people to walk her dogs so that she can get to her trainer. Others, desperate, rush harsh. Many people's kids climb in. Many pets assert the dominion of their drives. There's stretching and the taking of medicine. There's accounting and anxious text checking. There's scanning for bossy emails and preconceptions. Lists get made. For some, there is breakfast. Once spring rolls around there is running before the heat and catching the first shift sitting outside the punk bakery to smoke, drink coffee, and "break each other's balls" before work does what work does. I asked them about this phrase once and sparked a debate about whether it is properly "break" or "bust." Whatever, Professor, they laughed, yanking your chain, busting your balls, don't take it so serious!

Some people sleep in. Other people wake at the sun. Some people walk into the house and see only the order in it. Some people serve other people. Some use the quiet time to do the best things quiet time allows. Some people waste it, which is not the opposite of using it well. When I was little I had a task: to make coffee for the adults, measuring out the Maxwell House, setting the breakfast table. Then I'd leave for school and my early teachers would let me into the teachers' lounge. A little troll doll kid overhearing Allende, Planned Parenthood, and MLK. A confused and sunny face taking in the voices and the concept of concepts, before the day.

(DAVIS 2010; EIGEN 2004; HEJINIAN [1980] 2002; JACOBUS 1995; PEREC [1974] 2008)

Swells

We write to what's becoming palpable in sidelong looks or a consistency of rhythm or tone. Not to drag things back to the land of the little judges but to push the slow-mo button, to wait for what's starting up, to listen up for what's wearing out. We're tripwired by a tendency dilating. We make a pass at a swell in realism, and look for the hook. We back up at the hint of something. We butt in. We try to describe the smell; we trim the fat to pinpoint what seems to be the matter here.

Words sediment next to something laid low, or they detour on a crazed thought-cell taking off. I saw a woman standing on a sidewalk, chain-smoking while she talked to a buff younger man. She was trying to get him to give someone else a break because he means well or he didn't mean it. Maybe her son. "He don't know no better." She was hanging in there, but the whole top half of her black hair was a helmet of white roots. She was using her fast-thinking superpowers to run a gauntlet of phrases and get out quick even though we all knew she was just buying time.

A thought hits at an angle. Subjects are surprised by their own acts. But everyone knows a composition when they see one. A scene can become a thing after only a few repetitions. At the Walmart in New Hampshire, scruffy middle-aged men hang back at the register, letting their elderly mothers pay. The men have a hint of sour and the abject; their mothers are a worn autopilot. Women talk in the aisles about the local hospital; it's incapable; it misreads people, handing out exactly the wrong, killer drug.

(ERICSON 2011; SEDGWICK 1997; SEIGWORTH AND TIESSEN 2012; SERRES 1997; STEVENS [1957] 1990)

Dilations

The Hundreds is an experiment in keeping up with what's going on. Ordinaries appear through encounters with the world, but encounters are not events of knowing, units of anything, revelations of realness, or facts. Sometimes they stage a high-intensity tableau of the way things are or could become; sometimes strangeness raises some dust. This work induces form without relieving the pressure of form. It pushes and follows histories out. It takes in signs and scaffolds. If our way is to notice relations and varieties of impact, we're neither stuffing our pockets with ontology nor denying it: attention and riffing sustain our heuristics.

What draws affect into form is a matter of concern. Form, though, is not the same thing as shape: and a concept extends via the tack words take. Amplified description gets at some quality that sticks like a primary object, a bomb or a floater. The image that comes to mind when you read that (if images come to mind when you read) might not be what we're imagining—and we're likely not imagining the same thing either. Collaboration is a meeting of minds that don't match. Circulation disturbs and creates what's continuous, anchoring you enough in the scene to pull in other things as you go.

"Punctum" ought to mean whatever grabs you into an elsewhere of form. There ought also to be a word like "animum," meaning what makes an impact so live that its very action shifts around the qualities of things that have and haven't yet been encountered. You can never know what is forgotten or remembered. Even dormancy is a kind of action in relation. Think about watching a dead thing, a thing sleeping, or these words. Think about skimming as a hunger and defense against hunger. Think about the physiological pressure of itching.

(BARTHES [1980] 1981; DELEUZE [1988] 1993; FREUD [1925] 1961; GOFFMAN 1981; MASSUMI 2010; MOTEN 2013; NERSESSIAN AND KRAMNICK 2017; POSMENTIER 2017; SHAVIRO 2016)

Space Junk

Things cross your path like the fireflies you once dreamed of collecting in a jar. Memories come at you like space junk. My sister, Peg, remembers that our mother made us get short haircuts when we were kids because it was easier to take care of. All I know is that when my hair is cut short it's chaotic. I *remember* the humiliation of the high school yearbook picture with the parted hair all poofed up on one side. And that, only because the picture showed up at the bottom of a box forty years later.

Thought is an afterthought.

(A BOX OF PHOTOGRAPHS ONCE TAKEN; SISTER TALK OVER DECADES)

You have to start somewhere

I dreamed I was emptying the blue glass vases we bought for her memorial service at the Elks Lodge. I had learned long ago, following her around like a duck, that cleaning up was how you started a day or the labor of carrying on. But now I was alone in a panicked hollow act and I knew it. The flowers in the vases were brightly surreal, like plastic, but bloated, too, like a swollen Cabbage Patch doll face or a generative bacterial load blooming into a state of indistinction.

Then I was leaving her house. We had to go. We had to leave the little dog behind. I ran back in to put the laundry in the dryer, do something with the trash. I had a second thought about the kitchen. I could repaint the shelves, restock, replace tuna fish and lentils with tomatoes and McIntosh apples. The dream flared up at the judgment call. I panned the perimeter of the tree line, scanned the living room hankering at her jade tree, the blue Sandwich Glass teacups on the windowsills. The front door closed at the other end of the house, its sound precise like something momentarily proving true.

(BLUE GLASS VASES; MCINTOSH APPLES; TOMATOES)

This is vanilla

These prose poems come from a long poetic and noetic collaboration. The project pays attention to the relation of scenes to form, observation to implication, encounters to events, and figuration to what sticks in the mind. To convert an impact into a scene, to prehend objects as movement and matter, retains a scene's status as life in suspension, the way an extract in cooking conveys the active element in a concentrated substance that comes in a small brown bottle. (This is vanilla. *This* is almond.) The elaboration of heuristic form on the move points to pattern, patina, atmosphere: the object world of vestiges that scatters bumpily across the plane of what is also a vibrant tableau. But we get it: your eyes want a place to land on. You want to know what happened when the glances passed or where the train of a dark sentence will go. At different speeds we move around the effects, causes, and situational membranes. As we proceed we sift figurative types and object relations, seeking out the gists of things. Our styles move in proximity to currents. We get distracted sometimes. This is a practice of tightening and loosening the object-scene in hundred-word swatches.

(B. ANDERSON 2009; DIACONU 2006; FONAGY AND TARGET 2007; INGOLD 2015; MANNING 2009; MASSUMI 2010; QUICK 1998)

Handyman

He's helping her make the fox-owl for her genetics class, bending coat hangers into a ribcage, some wings, what kind of neck? *The Voice* comes on, she squeals, papers rustle, a tool crashes. In the living room, he perches on the hearth, his ears pricking on the first sign of a performer's bad pitch or throaty soar. The fox-owl hangs gracefully from his right hand. His fingers make the fox ears. He bleats when I skip the comments from the coaches—their sincerity tracks ("I love seeing you blossom, it does my heart good, me, me, me") or the long clips of the contestants' life melodramas bloating out of the detail of lost love, a house fire, poverty. Sitting in the living room, fox-owl in hand, all ears, he's a professional singer again, soul trained on the little tip that could drop from a coach's lips.

Sentimentality doesn't describe this noumenal-material suspension, the sudden cushioning density of the summons to an outside chance. Everyone has their own version of the glimpse of a long-forgotten realm of possibility suddenly intruding into the real like a splice of light captured in a photograph. My version of this is a recurring dream in which I'm walking to the back of an old house I forgot existed through room after room, repeating my surprise to rediscover them, some already clean, most still occupied by the detritus, clothes, and toothbrushes of a living that once looked for traction and company here.

A fantasy of a lit life is a worry stone to rub and it's a disturbance, too, even if it feels like comfort-food thought. We're gonzo for a minute. Then we'll see a chipmunk. He'll say it will be OK. I'll say you can get your sweaters out. There'll be four seasons again, and rain.

(DILLARD 1975; LINGIS 2015; *THE VOICE*)

Writing, Life

Once, I needed the perfect time and place to write. I stood in my way like a poison-pen letter to myself. But slowly, under the velocities of worldy reals that came and went, I learned to write in my own skin, like it or not.

Making money, making dinner, taking care of people and stupid shit, getting sick or getting well, getting into and out of what presented, I ended up with a writer's life. I learned to write in thirty-minute episodes on my frail mother's dining room table with a three-year-old playing with old plastic toys underfoot. I took notes on my phone at a doctor's office. I started the day writing in bed even though I had only ten minutes. Over time, I became allergic to the long-winded and roundabout, cutting words down to size. But then I'd become attached to a word fern shooting up in the space between words or I'd be surprised by something energetic already somehow taking off.

Some people have long, lean writing muscles; mine are shortened and taut like a repetitive stress injury turned into a personal tendency. I can write anywhere now but not for long, and it's only in the morning that I have that kind of energy and interest.

Things are usually in my way but that's the thing about writing. For me, it's an arc sparking in the midst of what's already freighted. It knots up on what crosses its path in a bit of bark, sparks on a sliver of rock, turns its back on someone.

For me, writing is necessarily recursive. Every day I start at the beginning, scoring over words like a sculptor chiseling things neither here nor there. Working words is like feeling out the pitch of a note set by an imaginary tuning fork. Pockets of composition can produce worlds as if out of thin air but only because writing is a compression stretched by a torque. When writing fails the relation of word and world, it spins out like car wheels in mud, leaving you stranded and tired of trying.

Deleuze once thought to say we're *for* the world before we're *in* it. Writing throws the world together, pulling the writer in tow into contact with a slackening, a brightening, a muffling. Something saturates with physicality and potential. There is a pond and then the occasional water bug skimming its surface.

(CLOUGH 2000B; DELEUZE 1986; DELEUZE AND GUATTARI 1987; KUSSEROW 2017; RAFFLES 2011, 2012)

Red Bull Diaries

To add insult to critical injury it was a chrome cylinder of diet Red Bull Zero that closed my throat despite its promise to lubricate the suicidation drive I call work. Even if it's just a job, what is just? It never releases, ever. The snake replaces the mole, the body converts to a trip wire for talk, and the bargaining is desperate freedom, which is to say, whatever, motherfuckers! I'm your teacher and I showed up. This week's *wah wah wah* translates as "use the object!" which is a spell to provoke a rhythm. The university is a harbor for Cartesian OCDers testing out their desires for impact.

TUESDAY

I was a good close reader as a child. At eight I made money for my mom at the track because I didn't rely on instinct, whatever the hell that is to a girl who'd had only a minute to look around before shaking her head purse-lipped. Ply me with a Shirley Temple and I'll tell you where to place your bets. Now I dope an hour before any event, risking a shut throat to keep me on top of the mouth where I promised *someone* to be. My heart is at stake—but fuck a sticky heart when there's a shot at a good long talk between a you and me.

WEDNESDAY

I and another loaf-thighed white woman are writing midafternoon in a bar. I don't know what her grimace is about, but I am imitating a friend who writes like her, hunched over a notebook with a cloudy sake to maintain an ironic line on sovereignty. This morning I awoke on my side in the dark and wrote with my thumbs for a few hours, breasts hanging clear of the open shirt. The ginger cat climbed onto my hip. Sometimes work is the most important thing, and sometimes it's like walking into a beautiful room and grinning at the weather. What would it mean to have that thought? Rain, snow, wind, sun.

THURSDAY (FOR SIANNE NGAI)

I sipped vodka with club soda and a twist and a ginger kombucha too because you told me that the combo produces frenzy like a speed high I'd gladly grind my teeth into niblets for. It is Thursday and everyone is taking things a little personally. A friend is having a tube slid up her thigh to fix a torn heart and another is sliding a tube through his nose to fix a distended gut. The adorable kids wearing Vans right near me are taking belly selfies and using phrases like "throw a blanket over it" to get the subject changed. I am trying so very hard to want the world I have in front of me to want. My heart is beating so fast that I swear I could beat the shit out of something quite grand with it. On Skype you miss the breakthrough dreaming that follows a series of sleepless nights: there's too much flicker and echo to grasp the whole psychotic show.

FRIDAY

Here's a story:

Once upon a time a dog wandering on the dirt took a shit that turned out to be a big baby crying from despair at its uselessness, and even though we knew that by the end everything would be OK because the shit would turn into compost, it was sad. These days even a shit has to enter the workforce. Even a flower petal is obliged to produce something. I have a darkish mind; I need half a break. There is no getting around the object, or unsaying a thing, or unseeing what floats by or sets for a spell.

("EVERYTHING IS GONNA BE ALRIGHT"; HOBBES [1651] 1991; HOMER 2016; KWON 2004; LAPLANCHE 1999; LINEBAUGH 2008; *PEANUTS*; SHIRLEY TEMPLE; WINNICOTT [1971] 1982)

As if

Thought images now touch matter as a matter of course. Composites of money, manipulation, and impact take on the cohesion of a milieu or a habit as if they're worlds to live in or want. Built environments have gone live in an all-sensory surround. Objects, deserted by the big baby subject who wants everything but can't leave itself alone, rise up like the undead; they raise a hair or stand proud in their texture like the nap of corduroy. Even the shape of things has to be defended. We want people to ask *what if*, but many are already full throttle into *as if*. Anything can seem like (or be) a game. An event is a loss of footing; the nightly news is an end times shoot barely covered by the gauze of the public eye.

Everyone's a sensitive now. Someone looks at you, a little slip shows up, you claim some way of living. Preppers have turned their apartments into survivalist storage units; they dream of living in a bullet-proof railroad car. Their daily leisure-time practices—canning food, shooting practice, more food canning, scouting for getaway land, shooting, fooding, scanning—are a way of breathing, as in take a breath. But now half of the top 1 percent are Preppers too. They know the instability rampaging inequality brings, that the food supply will go down with GPS, and finance with the internet, so they give to progressive causes but also stockpile gold, cryptocurrency, and real estate in New Zealand or a luxury condo in a nuclear-hardened underground missile silo tricked out with solar air filters, a tank to pick up owners in a four-hundred-mile radius, tilapia farms, a sniper roost. They get Lasik surgery because there won't be replacement contact lenses or glasses. They'll prevent cliques by rotating chores.

(THE BUILT ENVIRONMENT; THE NAP OF CORDUROY; OSNOS 2017; PREPPERS)

Checked out OK

Police reports in small-town western Massachusetts newspapers note residents' suspicions . . . a child reported home alone at the Brook Estates turns out to be an adult and OK . . . a man seen looking into car windows on Spring Street is a blind man just waiting for a bus. . . . A dangerous-looking animal moving about on a man's property is a black plastic trash bag blowing in the wind . . . threatening graffiti on the lawn is markings left by phone company employees warning of gas lines.

The precisions of what could be unfolding are a trail of bread crumbs opening onto unknown registers. There are four reports of men crawling in the middle of the road; one man seemed to be licking the road, another man seemed to be licking door locks on apartments on North Pleasant Street. A human hand in the middle of the road was just a rubber glove, a blood-soaked glove on Elm, just a pink glove. But the patterns of licking and hands in roads remain. Women report intruders who leave alien urine in their toilets, eat bananas, take four 60-watt lightbulbs, or four boxes of cranberry bread mix. Or a favorite white bowl is cracked.

A composition regrounds thought in a vivid pragmatics. A rhythm interrupted, or the shoot of an affect, are events in the variegated poiesis of a world riven by experiments. It matters that something was yellow, not red, that it passed in a blur, or something moaned. A bit of social debris, a scattering of material-aesthetic forms taken up or left to languish like litter are an archive of objects of attention. Regleaning them is a thought practice that needs materials to think with more than it needs the attitude-skill of debunking.

Thought can wait to feel out the recomposition of a tendon snapping back.

(CLOUGH 2000A; ERICSON 2013; FOUR BOXES OF CRANBERRY BREAD MIX;
STENGERS, MASSUMI, AND MANNING 2009)

Graduation Speech, 2016

During the last four years, people threw sex to the crocodiles. People smashed people into trees. People got fried, fired on, fired. People hated each other's likes. People wore plaid like their mothers' mothers, and put aviator glasses on dogs. On the chance that something good might happen, people called each other from cars.

We opened the window and dropped things out. There was more dancing than singing. We learned about uprisings but not about puns, because puns aren't considered knowledge. Meanwhile a local family was so poor it lived off cigarettes and apples. Then the black dad was beaten with arms like chains. Is scar tissue live or dead? Then the white perps appeared on the news stiff and proper in suits. What do you do with parents and nations once you've decided not to kill them back? Once you stay close to love, despite all the evidence?

Bearing angry beards and radical thinness, stop apologizing for wanting to live speculatively. While your hair's streaked and sharply undercut, please forgive your own desperate debt. Find the hole in every room; be queer as fuck. If not, you'll buy T-shirts to wear at the gym asserting variations on "there are no words."

It might be worth saying that the next phase pulses. We've done a lot of coasting in our life. We've coasted more than lived. The yogurt, the potatoes, the peanuts and bananas. If we're lucky, and only if we're lucky, we'll get to do more of that, more not paying attention and being forgiven for mistakes we could have avoided. But the world isn't made for most of the people who make value in it: rebegin there. That includes us. All the kissing and commenting and ridiculous eating to keep things going distract us: the exceptional cruelty too.

(CULLER 1988; FACEBOOK; INSTAGRAM; OCCUPY; STRIKE DEBT!;
WALLACE [2005] 2009; YUMMLY)

The New Ordinary

The new ordinary is a collective search engine, not a grammar. A table of elements flashes up erratically, throwing up a bit of atmosphere or a practice you may or may not take to. There are receptivity genres and they have consequences. In the uncanny mode, something surfaces eccentrically like the message of a Magic 8 Ball whose mystery meaning spurs thought's drift in search of the serious, or just drifts. In the slow-learning mode you start to get into a musical genre, then you start to notice all the insider references, or your foot starts to tap. There's always the question of whether others notice and what they know.

Things land on you, ending up in a facial tic or passing fast, a one-time-only smirk. The impacts on your body are seeds for a worlding. A phrase in circulation becomes your new jumping-off point. Or you find yourself suspended in a partially compelling form of eye contact, or a tendency to warm up to strangers that goes only so far. Some things etch into you like tree sap baked onto a windshield. Everyone puts in petunias on Memorial Day or grief over killed kids is the thing that has to be handled now. Identities are the expressivities of a situation—capacious performances and a work that has to be done.

The everyday is not a conceptual burial ground drumming things out of thought. More like an energy circuit scoring over all the incipient tendencies in a scene and what's actively taking form. Some people find methods of living out whatever's happening, some only sometimes, others just pace and chafe at the imposition. Everyone's got an angle. Some practice some kind of appetite control, others go with the flow as if it's just interesting to see what will happen next.

(A PHRASE IN CIRCULATION; KILLED KIDS; MAGIC 8 BALL; SEARCH ENGINES)

Contact Sheet

It is only evidence that she's been somewhere at the same time as her camera's been there. There's a pig in a doorway, a street, a man from behind. There are street crowds sweating and a glaring woman gesturing although she's alone. The place seems akimbo, as though wildly drawn by a child's tight fist. The problem of a book is that it is fixed. But "archive" points to a strewn thing scattered and prey to inattention, let alone winds and kicks. Will we want to know that insurgents at the skirmish wore brightly colored jeans? We can't forecast all of the archives into which this will slot, each according to its palate.

The contact sheet is a record of no memory. The images track lens cruising that hits a thick. Some details point elsewhere. Shoes are worn in many senses. It's all side effects, clattering with a few pricking moments. Sometimes it's blurry when the camera swerves or overfocuses. It's hard not to get vitalist about it; hard not to melodramatize; hard too not to slice the world into precious still lifes on a string. They were fighting with their fingernails, but there was no event? The revolutionary ordinary is contact and action inducing the speculative present.

The body is a contact sheet with a nervous system.

That girl in profile smiles and covers her lower lip with her teeth, which in the next frame emerge all stained and mottled, as though she had kissed herself with blood. Groups of people look around for prey or try not to be prey. There is an image of grinning at nothing you can be sure of. But not all the untimely is uncanny. Because presence isn't overpresence it can sit there like a meal's full feeling. To witness struggle is not always to be one with suffering.

You want to get the atmosphere. The caption states, "Someone was smoking pot." You can't help but breathe deeply while reading that phrase, wanting to inhale the head of the world. Doesn't revolt require lubrication and interruption—isn't that why it's sexy? RETURN THE WORLD TO

THE RAW. CHOOSE YOUR LAVA. WHEN YOU RUB SOMETHING ROUGH ON WHAT'S ROUGH IT GETS SMOOTHER. Politics moves across the surface like sex with its rush-hour friction and minor pulsation. If you skim the sheet—and there's no choice—you've only just arrived at its gist.

(BOLAÑO 2012; CADAVA AND CORTÉS-ROCCA 2006; MARX AND ENGELS [1848, 1888] 2008; MEISELAS 2015; TAUSSIG 1992; TAYLOR 2014)

The Things We Think With

Our citations are dilations, not just memories we have fidelity to. We meant for this text to appear like *A Lover's Discourse*, its stories couched in cascading cites. But Barthes could animate whole worlds with the word "Goethe," whereas our referential matter is too singular, various, and plenty. So the performance called format takes another route here, windup parentheses holding the things we think with: encounters, a word, a world, a wrinkle in the neighborhood of what happened, and reading we wouldn't shake if we could. Even if some cites look like direct sources, all things are indirect sources, in truth. Our ekphrasis is brash, approximate, edited, and feeling its way around. It's ordinary writing.

Not just sources: all things are indirect. We trained to be patient for implication and context. Food arrives: is it turned? Threats to confidence appear to appear. We overhear unruly talk that pulls us back. People *could* say, "We got remediated today: I feel so close to you now." *The Hundreds* crisps context and extends scenes. Its tropes are never mere. There is location, skin, convergence, and the fallout of failing numbness. The form knowledge takes involves limited reception. There is spareness and filling in.

(BARTHES [1977] 1978; W. J. T. MITCHELL, FORTHCOMING)

Worlds

Howie Becker said a world is real people trying to get things done, mostly by getting other people to do things. We look for applause in a collective activity no one wants but everyone tacitly agrees to. Like method actors, we try walking from the hip like that guy, or avoid eye contact on the sidewalk but mumble something in passing like them. Even Al Pacino has to follow strangers for months to get a mannerism right and becomes the character only as the curtain is going up. Roles are the practiced labors of being we copy from others; everything's in the perfect detail worked into a compositional stance. Jazz musicians are supposed to smoke dope; graduate students learn how to please their professors.

The social is a provisional movement psyching out the pros and cons of possible links and then doing things with them. There's no point in trying to get to the bottom of things when friends borrow a book or a shirt and then forget it's not theirs. And even if you try to go it alone, there's always a backlog of things you went along with or didn't pay attention to.

In the perfectly quotidian ambition to register what's happening, some things get re-upped and others don't—"She always wears red," "We don't drink with meals," "We love Vegas" (or film noir, or that restaurant, not that one). In the course of things, you send your kid to a new school, or you're a regular somewhere or from somewhere, you're homeless and racially, sexually marked, or you have a persona that reenacts the Civil War, or you're now in the habit of losing yourself every night in a serial immersion, or you get one of the available disorders, or any little thing now sets you off.

(GETTING IT, GETTING INTO IT; GOPNIK 2015; LAHR 2014; QUOTIDIAN AMBITIONS; SERIAL IMMERSION)

Weight of the World

A worlding is an imperial promise of a form barely roughed out and still charged with its own retractability. Hedging grandiose gestures at truth with the kinds of legibilities that lives in contact yield, it self-maps a potentiality out of an ecology of energetic precisions. A "we" likes hot food or it doesn't. A present lands. Characters rise to the occasion but also hope for a reprieve, sharpening our skills, tucking our tails.

Thinking goes sideways. Anything can start to act like a hinge, activating something suddenly somehow at hand. Forms piggyback on each other. One form moons another over its skill set. The incidental lives on as a facial expression or a skin sensation.

A stranger exchange is a flickering resource. In New England, you wouldn't think of calling attention to yourself by putting your junk out on the street; in Texas, that's just what you do, and it's not personal. Then you watch to see what happens. Someone who stops will look to see if there will be objections, some information, or a missing screw, some sign of good will or irritation. An opportunity stained with social weight spirals into all the social problematics.

We need the weight of the world we fear. We're selfie-obsessed or hoarding. Or we're all about mindfulness and hardened against those who fail. Whether we're jumpy, or trained in the controlled pause, it's a world under pressure that inspires us. We rage up from unsteady to overwhelmed or labor at athletic yoga that takes us all the way down every day. Too many get a shit storm of a life and then have to find a way to get to the food bank on top of everything. The rich criminals push through the sinking bodies, their own crazy now their only, lonely undertow.

(CLOUGH AND HALLEY 2007; LEPSELTER 2011, 2014)

Today in Political Emotions

Yesterday Kenny reappeared, a good guy who has just never been able to keep it together. He means to love like so many abusers, but when the walls close in that is what they do. He gets work, he works, he loves work, he gets mad, he pops off, he gets fired, and then he's back on the street in front of the CVS, until he gets work, works, gets mad, pops off, uses reason, pleads for a second chance, gets it but not a third chance, lands on a friend's couch until one day it's so humid the mice scream for air, and then the bicycle comes out to mow down people who look like they might give him a dollar. The campus police chase him too: he's black. His teeth look like an aerial photograph of the West Indies.

I told him I'd just mentioned him to Bush, one of the homeless ministers at my gym who live off the grants now thinning out because of the stuck state budget and Kenny said, quiet, I could use that right now. So this morning I went back to Bush and he started on what drugs is he, what stealing is he, what's his game, it was like a film where the shadow of a monster appears on the wall although the actor's body remains ordinary, unremarkable. I said, you were homeless once, what the fuck! and he went on about cheaters and I went on about how hard it is for the tried to try one more time and he said if Kenny called he would "diagnose" him and I said, I thought you were a man of God, not some kind of condescending cleaning machine. It was stupid and desperate for me to say. He promised fidelity, but by then my trust was slashed by a row of frenzied scythes.

Maybe I was quick to shred because of what else had happened upstairs. A stranger had stepped up on the lateral machine just next to my elliptical. After a while a "Me and Mrs. Jones" voice came up behind us, and said, "Hey sugar, I didn't know you came here!" And she said, "I do," and he said, "So what's been up?" She says, "help . . . help," all quiet, looking straight ahead without object. Her voice is flat, her face poised in exact parallel profile to mine. "Help, help." Like that. I say, "Do you need help, do you want help?" He says, "She doesn't need help, I wouldn't be like that!" I say, "When a woman says 'help, help' you've got to help her." She:

"Go on now and do whatever it was you came here to do," with no intonation at all, flat like those medieval chants where everything's equally weighted. She had to say it twice like that before he left. I said, "Is it OK that I said that? Are you OK?" "OK, OK, OK, OK." She kept on pumping, and after a minute I turned my face away. Soon she was gone.

On the way out I mentioned this incident to a staff member, I don't know why. She said the gym is tough; you just have to keep the tempers tamped down. She works part-time for the day care. "So many of the babies cry so hard, and if they don't calm down in fifteen minutes I have to call the parents to retrieve them." I got upset that even an infant isn't allowed to be inconvenient. She said, "That's why sometimes I break the rules, and give them twenty."

(*BIGGER THAN LIFE*; GAMBLE, HUFF, AND GILBERT 1972; MELOY 1998)

The Road

The American road is an infrastructural problem of a different order.

1. Once it ventured forth on the wings of the road trip and the family vacation. Giant roadside spectacles were its opportunistic gifts: the world-famous ball of twine, a towering milk bottle, a lug nut the size of a horse.

2. Its attachments/compositions: the billboard, the national park system, the motel, Kerouac, *Sunset* magazine, Route 66. Howard Johnson's had clam-strip dinners and mod furniture in orange and turquoise.

3. Its timing/frictions: after the Dust Bowl, the hobo trains, against the hard reals of economic drift and free fall, it declared it would be families traveling and they'd need toilets and running water.

4. Now the road's indifference is more morose. Its forward movement catches itself on the detritus of the big social project; it whirs a dull silence over sprawl; it asphalt-entombs/exhumes the matter poems of black bodies floating in city streets, brown bodies dead in the back of unrefrigerated semis.

5. Drug trafficking and racial profiling for privatized prisons are the growth industries it stages; privatized speed lanes concretize the mobility of money.

6. A few sparkle zones stand out against the badlands of blank strip malls and parking lots. That's what you see on a road trip.

7. Once I walked a Vermont road on a cold dark night. Footsteps were following me in the woods. Then the aurora borealis broke open the sky in purples and greens for twenty minutes.

8. One year, the winter broke New England's back, snow piles narrowing the roads to a half lane, treacherous turns at corners you couldn't see around, rooftops collapsing under the weight.

9. A visceral memory of dread is embedded in the highway drone outside my grandmother's house from long nights trying to get to sleep. It reminds me every time I hear it.

10. Yesterday, I heard a radio ad for a "live ride." The average car on the road is ten years old, so mostly dead rides. Drivers aren't doing well either; some are in a slow, impaired drifting, others are hard joy/hate riding. Car insurance went up thirty percent in Austin this year. Distracted driving, they said. There's texting but also all the uppers and downers make for a bad combination.

11. On Nextdoor, everyday videos circulate of thieves jumping out of their cars and running up to grab the packages left on a doorstep.

(HOWARD JOHNSON'S; KEROUAC [1957] 2012; *SUNSET* MAGAZINE; TSING 2005)

The State of Drift

On the open road, things calmed way the fuck down and suddenly my "life" came up as *this* trail traveled, that picnic stop, that tree. Impeckable Aviaries was still in the old storefront. I remembered peering through these cracks of the fence into a bamboo paradise, the double yellow-headed and lilac-crowned Amazons in Victorian birdcages (though this is suspect since I don't actually know what they look like). In the tourist-trap cabin next door, the wooden dresser in the corner smelled like prairie, the black cast-iron picture frame swung on two little arms.

By the time we got to Fredericksburg I was picking out the houses I'd stayed in: the immateriality of two days here, the stone wall in that kitchen, that grass in that yard. The scenes were wound tight between then and the ends that were coming. A "dishwasher wanted" sign at a bakery where mugs with regulars' names on them hung from hooks set off a picto-fantasy of a little life for a little while.

We entered the West talking about failed relationships, picking up the threads after pit stops. Out there it was all stars, the darkness a full-on black. We jumped at the sudden clarity of a burro on the side of the road and again at the deafening croak of a hundred frogs on the walk to find dinner. We hit Big Bend early, the sun on a jackrabbit. We got stuck behind a driver so far into it that he never even registered us behind him. He was chewing gum. He was talking to someone in the passenger seat. He was turning his head from side to side like a Scantron. I could have honked, tried to get around him, but by then I was deep into an even keel, amazed by everything, including him.

(IMPECKABLE AVIARIES; SCANTRON; STERN AND STEWART 2016)

On Collaboration

We wrote back and forth with variable commitment to active uptake: we are separate people trying to stay in sync and to take in what isn't, to work with the heat of a proximity that echoes, extends, or hesitates into forms of life. Our bumpers are the archives we push off from. "Active uptake" was Michael Warner's phrase for how we enter a public through capture by its circulations; we become ourselves both more alive and tired at all kinds of speed. The impact that fires mutual awareness somewhere might figure as a thrilling link, an uneven curb, or persist like a conversation's low-hanging fog. Sometimes, a friend says, we wish that your texts would resist us more. Because, we respond, then you can feel that your reading is heroic. We're interested in what's active in receptivity. Active has no opposite. Even the easiest sentence is a test once you ask the background knowledge to come to the phone.

In any collaborative relation there is a fear of deep checking in. What do we do in the event of the force of clashing taste? It might turn out that we were falling through ice after all, not making tracks in the same-enough way. Some collaborators seek a secure job as the referent. The mind threatens to grow into an insane place if it's not getting to feel how it was supposed to feel. Some collaborators demand that everything confirms the circuits of their enjoyment. We are interested in the elaborate strange logic of the world. Being in the scene that is pulsating, not separating what's out there or in us. Without the plane of consistency, a series will often appear in tangles without syntax or as lines shooting out because the implication is on a frequency. A politics can be articulated in this difficult situation: these days we're panicking about causality; sensing mass mania, mass exhaustion, asthma; the distribution of borders and death and confused, upended life; the panic at what's fracking people in their bodies.

So we look for points of precision where something is happening. We don't presume what's going on in a scene but look around at what might be. We tap into the genres of the middle: récit, prose poem, thought experiment, the description of a built moment as in *The Arcades*, the Perecian exercise, fictocriticism, captions, punctums, catalogs, autopoetic zips, flashed scenes, word counts.

(W. BENJAMIN 1999; DAVIS 2010; DELEUZE AND GUATTARI 1987; GIBBS 2005; GLADMAN 2016; HARNEY AND MOTEN 2013; MUECKE 2008, 2016; PEREC [1974] 2008; STERN 2001; WARNER 1991)

The Icing on the Cake

I am the girl who sits by the fire whether or not it's cold. The three kids at the next table are clearly siblings, stealing gleefully from each other's plates. They have similar haircuts and their eyebrows are noticeably thin. They are young and their teeth are tiny squares. One kid is having a birthday and a large cupcake with a lit candle approaches. There is oohing and clapping, then high-spirited bad singing. After the silent beat of the child's wish they all blow because everyone wants in unison to wish that the wish would have a shot at coming true.

Draw a storyboard of this scene.

Does "birthday cupcake" suggest a budget or a festive surplus? How big is large? Are the surrounding tables paying attention or passively penetrated by the family's sound? Is it sunny out? What are the genders and races of these children and their muffin-delivering adults? How big or cropped is their hair? Are they all dressed alike, or do generations shift? Are there presents on the table? Are these the right questions? What is it about icing that links it to joy, to empire and excess and the sovereign tongue? Seriously, what is it?

(LOEFFLER 2017)

Bad Feelings

I fall into step on the sidewalk behind a family of five. The thin, blond grandmother has the gnawed face of a meth addict. She lopes when she walks, swinging her legs out and forward, cutting her eyes over her shoulders, arms circling a little randomly. It's as if she'd been torn limb from limb and now finds herself at the outlet mall with her daughter's family. Her shorts are ironed, she has nice sandals.

She reminds me of a woman I met who has trouble being in a room. I stood next to her. We started off pretty well, talking about books and travel and how we knew people, but after twenty minutes we were trapped. I drifted away, releasing us. Over the next three days, we ricocheted off a backlog of social failures; there were furtive looks, the occasional sharp turn on the poolside pavement to avoid contact. No bad feelings but bad feelings were between us, suturing us in a contact aesthetic like my childhood visits to the piano teacher—the earthy oils she wore, the way she ran her hand up the page of music, opening it flat without catching her skin on the staples.

(CONTACT AESTHETIC; CONTAGION; GIBBS 2006, 2011; PINE 2012, 2016)

Halloweens

A carnival atmosphere reigns at the neighborhood school today, and kids run around the way they do every day but wearing brighter colors and fearing, I can feel it, disappointment on the other side, a dulled thread pulling them into knowing that it's all difficult, that they are difficult, that their relations and the chocolate in the candy bag are not really very delicious. A disappointed tongue is one thing. The optimistic and knotty collaboration that is the Halloween costume, another. Some adult loves, hates, facilitates, or pragmatizes a child's wish. And there it is, a thing that will be repeated.

A woman lugs a bowling ball right up to her neighbor's lawn and rolls it hard from between her legs, just like when she was little. Maybe they won't notice the defeated garden or the bent fence? She's overcome by the sight of her action: her face grows slow, cabbagy. Shadows move in a picture window beyond the lawn's carpet, dull to the event that has not yet become one. An act can never be withdrawn. On the street behind her the Halloween festival goes on. The poor kids come early and stay late rubbernecking, hungry and also lingering.

(ARENDT 1958; MAVOR 2012)

Take a Breath

You take a walk. Something incipient but weighted throws together around you. One walker with a routine arms himself with giant headphones and a stick, another stays alert for a quick response to comments from passersby. The questions are basic, like what to do with your eyes.

One day, Ronn is walking Copper, our ancient dachshund runt, on a busy Austin street. A man in a truck waiting for a light to change calls out in an Irish brogue: "What a *beau*tiful dog." And then, maybe because he notices that the whiteness of her face is age, not a miracle, that her eyes are blind black with cataracts—she's not what she once was—he revs up his proclamations. "She's the most b*eau*tiful creature I've ever *seen*." Ronn is a little taken aback, but he's on it. "Thank you very much! She's a doll." He would have gone on, stepping up to the opening, but the light changed. I imagine the two men gazing at each other for a few seconds as their paths pull apart, interrupting something set in motion.

Another Ronn story (he likes to talk to animals): "I'm buttoning up my shirt and all of a sudden I smell this smell and there's this soft poop at my feet and Copper's standing there looking up at me like (shrugs his shoulders and stares with a deadpan 'Hooray for me and fuck you')." Ronn walks away, a little jaunty now, putting a point on his story as he goes. I'm the slightly giggling cowitness and not the judge.

Once I was walking our other dog, Kuka, past the schoolyard. A young boxer ran up to a man whose dog was on a leash. The man yelled, "Hey! Get your damn dog!" The boxer's owner was cavalier, slowly turning to amble over from the other side of the field. He called out way too casually, as if it wasn't necessary to say anything at all, "He's friendly." The worked-up guy included me in his retort. "*We* don't know that! Get your fuckin' dog, don't give me that shit." Now he was bouncing up and down and moving fast-forward like a beach ball blown by the wind. I was a little worked up too, fashioning reactions in my head: "Yeah, that's right!" or "Hey, leave me out of this!" Amazing how a dog loosed in public can set a man bouncing, but also, he sounded like he was from New England. That explains *some*thing.

Ethnography's commitment to writing from the ground is an impulse to stay open to what's in your vicinity. But the "ground" is not just a backdrop or a context; it's the sensed social-material-aesthetic atmospherics resonant in a scene, the threshold onto worlds of expressivity in a problematics. It's what sends people bouncing at the drop of a hat or sets off a line of associations at the sound of an accent. It's what's already taking off, a space where dogs sometimes master the art of deadpan.

(B. ANDERSON 2009, 2016; DOG WALKING; EXPRESSIVITY THRESHOLDS; GENERATIVE MISPERCEPTION; MCCORMACK 2013; THE ETHNOGRAPHIC GROUND)

Friction

On one side of the café January (they talk at length of her name) is on a date with a sweet internet hookup whose fingers are like Tiparillos. And it's going so great for a while until January says no, in a slightly louder voice, NO, I do not eat meat, it makes me feel bad, I won't even have plants. The guy loves meat. It's the only reason I see my father, he says: no one cooks meat like him. The conversation gets quiet and then turns toward work, and phrases like "and whatnot" spring up, so things get sweet again.

I have eight pairs of khakis and eight shirts, he says, so I never have to make a decision. My underwear is all sorts of colors, but that doesn't mean anything, she says—I like to live simply—and to look at her metal T-shirt and sweet flats with jeweled skulls embroidered on them, I get it. They are trying to maintain. They already know how they will fail because when they're not alike their jaws get set. Santa over here wants to give them five pouches of patience and some Xanax to help them ace the test like in fairy tales.

Outside, in the sun, a couple who divorced a year ago has a date to take an "inventory." Before the woman arrives the man tells a friend he runs into that it's been a year since he's seen his ex: they've kept it to email. The friend nods and backs off. The remainder tilts back in his chair, straightening up when she arrives in a van. She is a foot taller than he is: wider too. There is no awkward hug, just the scraping of metal chairs. Both are gray-pale, as though they'd remained inside since the apocalypse poisoned the air.

Each ex has a paper with penciled notes—I'd bet anything that their mediator, or someone's shrink or sponsor, suggested this tool so that they could erase their bullshit if it showed up for a fight. From the outside they seem tired. The woman is wearing big metal jewelry and the man a baseball cap backward. I'll begin, she says.

1. I was a narcissist.

Then quiet. Things have gotten so bad, she rebegins, that I had to do an inventory with another friend too, and she made me admit it: I'm all about my own feelings. The guy gets sad and seems humiliated, too, that still, a year later, he is profoundly passive in the air of her. He makes supportive noises.

1. I had my stuff, too, he mutters, looking at the paper. I tested you. We played games, she said. I wasn't trusting, he said.

2. Also, she said, I owe you money, I took a lot from you when you were sleeping, and she hits the table with a crushed ball of bills that scatter to the ground. Everyone on the outside rises and laughs, pretending to steal what wasn't ours, or theirs.

(JACKALOPE COFFEE & TEA HOUSE)

The Game as Method

The game is a form of life coming into being, extension, and activity, the blinking at the start of the day and the beyond to anything to be explained. If I run out of gas but not out of love, if you let a piece go without completion, if the session's not finished but definitively over, if the delicious coffee would only wake us forever, if we could come forth as "I" with the other objects, if we could take in that all things don't happen for a reason, if the flat voice were other than trauma, a failing. If you could be the kind of person you'd go out with again, if we could host the accusations we've flung around, if I could see sugar, labor, and resting as questions, if we could take unforeseen touch with soft eyes and no flinching, if you could stop-motion the arbitrary, if they could bear the common structure like vomit or accident, if we could take the fatal hit that it is all brevity and struggle, if the form of life turned toward a way of life and on the lips of our heads the present fell open, if we were game.

(COHEN 2011; FOUCAULT 1997; HEJINIAN [1980] 2002; KOESTENBAUM 2011; LACAN 1991; MALABOU 2011; MULLEN 2002; SPAHR 2005, 2011; SUTHERLAND 2009; WITTGENSTEIN 2009)

Once

In the fifties, mundane forms of care formed a scaffolding of relays people becoming middle class couldn't quite claim as their own. New habits stood proud as if they were judgments held in common. There was spaghetti day, laundry day, vacuuming day, a week of spring-cleaning. You lined up the kids to go food shopping, you made meals with one green and one yellow vegetable every night. A phone call during dinner always got the same response: "I'm sorry. We're having dinner. Could I have her call you back?" Tips circulated. Gadgets came and went. Scenes of pleasure floated by. Every night they listened to the nightly news.

The world had become something to see. A life had become something to have. There were family vacations at the lake, rowboats, the women on chaise lounges, the near-glamorous intimacy of those bathing suits. Winter clothes went into cedar chests for storage. Plaques mounted on walls went for the commonplace: "It's not the mountains ahead that wear you down, it's the grain of sand in your shoe." Our mother's dresser had a jewelry box and a milky blue statue of the Virgin Mary that glowed when the lights were turned off.

One of the things my partner, Ronn, and I have in common are the round, silver-rimmed glass ashtrays scored on the bottom with ridges in a design between a snowflake and an abstract geometric pattern. His parents built their dream house in 1952. It had seven closets; the unheated one became the root cellar. Later, they converted the garage into an office for their manufacturer's representative business.

By the time Helen died, after fifty-one years of marriage, Pop's house stood as an infrastructure of an upright life. The same can opener still mounted on the kitchen wall, a special tool to core a tomato or a strawberry. Tiny white glass bowls for the potato chips that occasionally replaced the oyster crackers with the soup at lunch. He kept an inventory of the food in his freezer in the basement: barbecue sauce (1), chili beans (1), chicken broth (5 quarts), yellow squash (2), green peppers (1), mixed greens (17), vegetable soup (14), turnips (4), deer sausage (1), deer steak (2), chicken legs, long (10), chicken legs, short (8), pork ribs (2), sirloin steaks (1), sweet potatoes (22), biscuits (30), rolls (1 box), sugar cake (1), turkey and broth (3), spaghetti sauce (27).

(1950S WOMEN'S BATHING SUITS; GLASS, SILVER-RIMMED ASHTRAYS)

This isn't consoling

One minute you're coasting happily, which is to say not coasting but
enjoying the feeling of coasting minus taking it for granted, and the next
moment it is gone and you were always the *bad dog!* of a universe of rules
and judgments. You worry this knowledge until it breaches the ordinary
with what might be an event or might, like most things, be healed by
secondary intention. Not knowing until later what will have been easy
and what will have been hard, what's a weapon and what nothing, what's
an extraordinary or ordinary touch, what's a sneeze or sickening.

In the middle

Most people seem to be in the middle of something they somehow ended up in. What's happening's provocations propel us and drag on us. Sometimes an offbeat chanting wants things decided one way or the other (is it work or play, good or bad, up or down?) as if the diffuse environmentality of things is itself a threat or too much to handle. Some worry that any opening is also an opening for power that's always on the prowl for its next victim.

Everyone's got their stories lined up—litanies of injustice tangled in the crazy or the funny. My Santa Cruz shuttle driver started in with how he and his buddies got a rental house by showing up early and offering to do a major landscaping job and paint the whole place as part of their rent. They did it all in the first two months. He liked to work all the time; he got that from his father. His first job was flipping burgers at McDonald's but he burned his arm bad on the grease after only forty-two dollars' worth. He liked being a manager at a Ross Dress for Less until a customer spit in his mouth and hit customers with a shoe. One of the customers was so impressed with how he handled himself he gave him a job selling cars, which he liked until the new owners started whiting out commissions on his pay slips. Now he drives shuttle, Uber and Lyft, and he likes that too.

There are ways of being up for all this that no one really wants: splintering tunnels of how-to advice, ways of regulating yourself with mindfulness or drugs, or speed shifts to stay in sync with a quick-shifting tempo-participation. A life ecology bloats with remedial labors: the constant straightening up, the compulsion to grasp at straws, the need to retreat, the little jokes that mark social contact, the nested troubles multiplying, the resentments slowly accruing.

The social is a charge of free radicals that have to be carefully selected, like the guests at a dinner party, or sharply scheduled like the ten-minute mandatory time-out every hour at the swimming pool just to be safe. It's an allegation paranoically aimed at you if you're the wrong color. It's an arraignment for those wearing really old shoes or sending out a vibe of defensiveness or judgment, even if it's accidental. The things that can make you or someone else the target of a war-mongering eye are so prolific and twisted that no list ever gets it.

Maybe there was a moment when all this became widespread. Thomas de Zengotita says the Kennedy assassination permanently tipped life into the surrealism of what just couldn't be true. Or people think modernism did something, or the industrialization of experience, or cognitive capitalism now, or the way media pull us into one little thing and then another. There's always talk of the fifties, or the thirties.

Meanwhile, back on the academic ranch, there was the time when social constructionists so locked onto the mediation of everything that *its* broken record became theirs, as if that was enough said. Humanist critique just keeps snapping at the world as if the whole point of being and thinking is just to catch it in a lie. As if some fixative of state power or normative fantasy could be the *only* problem and there's always something wrong with other people. Some of the things this view misses: all the extensions of ways of being touched, what it feels like to be carried along by something on the move, the widespread joking, the voicing, the dark wakefulness, the sonorousness, how managing a life vies with an unwitting ungluing, how things get started, how people try to bring things to an end, like the day, through things that slam or slide down their throats, why thought might become an add-on or take the form of a speed list, or why it matters that attention sometimes slows to a halt waiting for something to take shape.

We find speculative possibility not in dead matter or hypervalent structure but in rhythms interrupted, the shoot of an affect, trouble brewing in a posture.

(DE ZENGOTITA 2006; WAYS OF BEING UP FOR IT)

Cover Story

On an impulse you watch a stream of water bleed off the counter, which is what writing the present amounts to anyway, a scroll fighting off its own tears. Comedians call it commitment to the joke when the mind shadows itself and tries to push through to the front with an acrid hospital-room cheer. Tragedians and ideologues click along this arc looking for satisfying machines. But it's all a cover story: you can't say everything, even if you wanted to. You can't get to the bottom of things, just at the thick of them and the gravity that pulls them, and you, along. Yet the spike of attention from the rise of interest is only a certain kind of open.

It's like the adrenaline-coasting your body does when you dent a newly purchased car, launching it forever as a loser's possession. Then maybe you find a way to reattach to life, or it's the last straw. You can always shrug. You could notice that on the horizon there's sunlight and the world running toward you, and that's a happiness that will more than do. Some people slot kids into that scenario and others other things, and others nothing. It's all dilation, distraction, specifying attention. Daily we see things like that, like the guy at the reception hovering over his plate of food to protect it from the preying world. Or that look on someone's face because they *knew* they shouldn't wear that shirt. Or when your protesting mouth recalls the sharp hate of a child speaking with a limited vocabulary. Even if you're not free all the way through you can build from the space where you're not entirely crushed. Writing that requires composition and repetition, and the expanded time for untangling fresh extensions from the never quite vanquished complications.

In the cut ‾

In writing condensed, we amplified through subtraction, tightened up thought through a detour, leaching words. A new sentence arrived just because it had seven words. We were trying to make theory descriptive. We became differently averse to reductions and foreclosures, to certain namings of politics or the real. At times, the privileging of representation or ontology would set us off. Some poems pursued the collapse of dissociation and association. There were sharp cuts, a surprise funny. Others tried to align words to the conceptuality of ordinary things, to build muscles of response to the suggestion of a color or tone.

What Does *Webster's* Say about Soul?

Everyone in this café is casual—the whole neighborhood is, except at 5PM, when the shiny-haired businessmen arrive to delay going home. At the next table two women and a man are wearing pretty much the same jean and sweater outfits. One woman's hair is tousled faux-carelessly and the other's is drawn into a ponytail; the man sports a baseball cap. Ponytail opens a large white box, inside of which are three perfectly round cakes, frosted white: a wedding is being planned. One cake is covered with the white sugar pearls we associate with festive decoration, the kind of thing that like life is supposed to taste good but might break your teeth. One woman tastes the cake and the other talks and waves her hands. The man gestures toward the tousled blond as if to say her happiness is all that matters. The salmon sweater of the consumer has more texture than the green cardigan of the provider. Pictures are taken of the three cakes to send to someone's mother. The baker wants to know if the cake will go onto a stand. She gestures at face height and higher. The couple furrows its brow at the gesture, the future.

(SCOTT-HERON 1970)

Against literal-minded explorations of the ordinary

So, you're writing. You make a pass at capturing something or tagging along. It's too fast for you, it doesn't cooperate, but you get something, backing up at the hint of precision, muscling your way in. You see how much you can't catch, especially now that you're onto a composition of your own. You need another detail, you get rid of a container concept that doesn't work. Writing's mechanics of expansion and contraction change the concept's environment. Thought becomes a little surprised to latch on to something, to arrive somewhere, and still looks around, testing what flashes up a surround.

(MCLEAN 2017; PANDIAN AND MCLEAN 2017; RAFFLES 2011, 2012; TAUSSIG 2011)

At the Y

At the Y the young hungry boys ask for money because young hungry boys are hungry. If you say, "Do I know you?" they laugh and stay your friend. That means helping with their homework and buying chips and being teased. "I don't know why there are story problems about trains," one kid said. If he hits the vending machine just right he can get two bags, but that is nothing compared with the friend's friend who broke into a bakery last week and sold the cakes on the street for ten bucks a pop. The hundred they scored went for sliders and weed; he bought me a granola bar with the remains. "No worries," he kidded. A slider has a hole smaller than the slider. How many sliders will fill up his hole? Should he eat one now or save one for later when the hole knocks ferociously at the door?

Sometimes the resonance of a thing builds your strength even though nothing appears to be changing. One exercise involves a heavy rope wrapped around a pole that won't move. The rope is black and twisted, and the rough knots at the ends that you hold on to are huge, as though you grasp a giant's hands. The exerciser picks up the two knots. He is instructed to pull in his stomach until belly meets back. He begins pounding the large ropes on the floor. The undulations are profound. It's "Jack and the Beanstalk" loud. Maybe twenty-five thrums. Then rest. Then twenty-five more lashes of the rope, then rest. During the rest period people shoot the shit. Did you know masters licked their slaves' skin to establish the high quality of their sweat? Someone reads this from their phone, and we all make protest groans. The kids run after each other with their weaponized tongues jutting out. When they're gone Ty tells us that his grandmother's just passed, so we get respectful, quiet. The crazy mourners are getting to him. There's a sentimental heroin addict who steals dough from the pile of coats. I say my family has a guy like that: the histrionic are the most destructive. But then: you can't judge people when they're mourning, they've got a hole in them that big. I touch my thumbs and forefingers the size of a baloney. He says yeah, forgive me Jesus, I'd like to beat his ass. Then more thrumming.

There's a SilverSneakers club downstairs marked by the red-winged Mercury image with those parentheses around the wings that signify flight. Old-people gossip fills the common areas with pleasure and resentment howls. Black men in their loose brown clothes and women of all kinds hang there, and Asian men if they play chess, and grandbabies if the day care's closed. Once I asked them if I could have a cup of coffee before I went upstairs, and they said, "You don't get to ask that," and that was the end of talking till one day they asked me, "Hey, what's the rush, ghost!" I said, "I thought maybe you thought I was a little too white and university," and they laughed and said, "We know you! We know you!"

Every so often the women sitting around the locker room say, "I don't give a shit!" Giving no shits, no fucks, such searing phrases: is this what '68 left us? Their voices get a little loud when they say it, which is why I had to take note. A woman at work was bothering one of them. Another woman at work returned from the hospital, and she was so ashy she looked like drywall. Men around them were taking credit for their work, and the women got together and made some HR noise, same as at the church when the pastor was ogling the babies. People aren't easy even when they are, because they might trip you up, break your neck, or look away disgusted. But there's some give. Minute by minute, listening, advice, and business cards from the people working from home. The prosperity gospel is on. I get here when the only people working out are students, the old and otherwise unemployed, the self-employed and mommies, but by the time I leave the postwork crowd has arrived. It's February 15, and the mood's a bit depleted, the scale avoided. Blood and love share a vowel sound. The room is dank, humid.

In the mornings everyone talks about the president and someone says, I wish he would just shut up and be a president. We are all writing imaginary letters. Today I was thinking about the sentence "Why should you be spared?" I imagine buying prestamped postcards. I imagine gloves that shield my fingerprints from detection. I imagine setting up every day and writing, WHY SHOULD YOU BE SPARED?

(BROOKS [1945] 1987; CANTET 2001; "JACK AND THE BEANSTALK";
PUAR 2012; WILLIAMS 2005)

No world beyond the world

I was walking on the beach in San Diego. I saw a young woman dancing with a whip that might have been a length of kelp. She was wielding it like a lasso as she ran; then she'd crack it on the wet sand, her moves a little awkward but like a dancer's. When I was long past her the cracks of the whip got much louder, like a gunshot or a firecracker. In that weird relation of sound to distance, and because a thought-encounter's options remain in the air, I kept turning to make sure it wasn't something bad, and I could never catch her in the act, the whip always already sliding back. Then a young woman came out of the surf making eye contact with me.

"Does she have a whip?"

"Ya, I don't know if it's kelp? She's dancing with it."

"Dancing? I thought someone was throwing poppers at me."

"Ya, it's so loud now."

"Well, OK then, good, as long as you got up close and personal with her."

"Exactly. That's that then."

We grinned at each other.

The shared recognition of this whatever made us happy when we turned it into an attitude game.

(ATTITUDE GAMES)

Slide

A thought slides out of a story, overflowing the eddy of its liquidity. We mark out an elsewhere rather than arrive.

For us, a concept is a space that got lit up and lights up. We try to conjure up the world of its words and the words of its worlds.

Writing allows for anything to be a concept's matter or a matter's concept. Nothing guarantees it, but everything initiates.

We try to picture the energetics of thought/matter's movement, its sheering. Take New England red: Indian paint, barns, maple leaf, brick, chapped lips, a cardinal in snow, a face beaten.

Two Elizas

BETH

Her iron was low and her sugars were high. She fell asleep during conversations because she could not not, but also because the white and civilized noise of the world was no longer to be borne. She had spent her life intensely straight. She had worn classic clothes and assumed a posture that would shame a chair. Lovely asleep. One could love her creased cheek, except that it was so finely faded it seemed always to radiate the ending that impended. Till the end she had her hair straightened and colored the sheen of the extinct light brown M&M.

BIDDY

Her best friend was Princess Grace's first cousin so she was referred royalty. She looked twenty-one when her friends looked sixteen. She had cheerleader breasts and a parenthetical ass. She was a Beverly Cleary heroine who'd known no reversals, the kind who was nice to homely girls, with a big impersonal smile. People who grumble through the world cannot give a big impersonal smile. Hers was like a free brownie or a dollar found on the street. The ordinary is an ocean that moves for the lucky, whose ridiculousness remains a secret so open that it remains a secret.

Keep It Together

You have to keep your wits about you. You might learn to catch a passing quip or to turn your head away. There are chances for sincerity or snarkiness. There are receptivity mistakes, maybe the poise of a balancing act, at best, the fluidity of a perfect timing.

I'd heard that the men at the Ellacoya Store were so right-wing it would make your head spin, so I expected them to be all puffed up and prickly when I walked in, but they were wide open and mid-grin. We were from Texas. "Texas! What a shit hole. Those people are nuts. If they can't see a hundred miles in every direction they're miserable. . . . This guy visiting here hated the *trees*; he said they were always in the way." We knew we were toying with stereotypes and first impressions, but that was the game. "Amarillo! That place is like the surface of the moon. If there was oxygen on the moon those people would all move there."

They had moved up to New Hampshire from little run-down mill cities in Massachusetts because they just liked it better. But then came the "but." "But this is a Gestapo state. Don't drink and drive in this state. They'll take your license." And there it was. It took three minutes to get to the right wing others shook their heads about. They were calling out some milieu I couldn't get into, but I could feel the force and fear of something going on with the police. It was like life was a set of roadblocks cooked down to a rage, and it could ignite faster than thought when provoked. But here, at the store, these guys were giggling their way through their coffee like they were floating downstream on a river of shit.

(HOLLY HUNTER)

Welcome to the Joke

Democracy kills me and kills you, but it's not always the same death we die or do. Why bother calling it rat poison if it would kill us too? I like to play with high and low. What I'm saying is that I've been in a lot of elements. Yesterday at the bus stop a fellow creature the gym ladies call "that particular element" asked for a hand—out, job, shake. That's the door bearing pussy in public means walking through. Manners are in the neighborhood of rules you can get shot for disobeying around here, but mostly it's ice cream on the sidewalk and shrugging.

One stop is a concrete utopia. The chairs squeak loudly and the twisting kids love the unbearable music of their own butt power. They don't have a clue about humorlessness. They get fried, then they're happy. They hate change and whine from boredom. They enjoy cheesy starches and suck their yogurt out of brightly colored tubes. Charlie, want a chicken wing? No thanks, A HOT DOG, I TOLD YOU! But you can dip it in the sauce just the way you like! He runs to the river and holds on to the fence as though it bars a freedom he can feel. He is smiling, not wanting. Older couples also try to get some heat on here. The old coot sitting two tables down meets a big blond with grand arms and a fancy leather bag that could hold a whole roasted chicken. He's bored. He looks over and asks if I've read about debt. He wonders how people bear the pressure of it. He tells me he's seventy-five and was raised by depression-era parents to avoid debt like the plague—but nowadays it's just expected. I say, maybe people don't believe in later; maybe they just believe in keeping now afloat. He's handsome and silver, no fat on him. I ask if he wants some water: I have extra. He says, "I'm drinking wine in the middle of the day because my liver's stopped working and why the hell not."

A lot happens out here, so many mouths opening and closing, so many flavors gone, and gone, too, all the kisses parents give to their children's sticky hands, not dead, not nothing, but not things you can whip out later in the attempt to star-date life.

Later it's Friday at seven thirty and three times in twenty minutes low-blood-sugar left-turners cut me off in their late-model hurry. Maybe it matters to get somewhere. Maybe they promised this time to be timely but left late; maybe they fear the passive wrath of their friends, who will now have to mill around some loud hot room waiting for a table to open and it's Friday after work when people like to stop discerning time. A belated beauty knows she'll be welcomed, but even she speeds around the corner with that deadpan face of a bad driver. A sudden parking spot makes the traffic jump and spray recklessly around a stopped Civic. At the bar a boy steps over to compliment my stout. He tells me he's in sales now and misses the office—over there are the people he left behind. Go back, I suggest. You can never return, he says. I have to relearn life all over like a baby, *it's damn lonely*. On the highway overpass teenagers stand waving late into the night. Maybe a driver will get caught up in their joy and rear-end a semi. Maybe all the auto pilots will be so anxiously texting they'll confirm that the mechanical's encrusted on the living.

(BERGSON [1900] 1914; NGAI 2015; POSTONE 2004; *STAR TREK*)

The women

The women in customer service ask me, "512, is that an *area* code? From Texas? Oh, my, I feel sorry for people who have to live there, what is it now: tornadoes, floods, and what's the *temperature?*" As New Englanders, they also believe in social services, so not Texas. But what's happening here is a national conversation lite about living right in the middle: not too much of this, not too little, not too far, not too close. It's as if everyone's joined the local booster club, and, for a minute, excess and the sad are somewhere else. It's a deliberate collective fiction that leans into a joking but also squares on a straight-up loyalty to the good that's in between.

Pete's daughter, Penny, drops into a chair at the kitchen table for a visit because she thinks Peg and I are a trip. She says she has to get back to work, but she's getting a beer. She's working for a defense attorney doing his shit work until she gets clients of her own. Some asshole beat the crap out of his girlfriend and Penny's come up with an argument that the 911 call is inadmissible because the statement "he choked me" is not an imminent threat but a past threat. She hates the work, but she's getting a charge out of the game. Part of me wishes I weren't here, but I've never been inside a lawyer's head before. Peg, though, has had enough of all *this*. She responds to whatever people say with, "Ya, I get that" just a split second before they've finished their thought because she knows where it's going. She's signaling a kind recognition, a being on their side, but also a wise-ass, Buddhist, disavowal booby trap that says let it go, zip it up, move on, that's enough of that.

We were in the state liquor store stocking up on tax-free social liquor for the summer. For fun, I asked my twelve-year-old to carry a big bottle to the register. The clerk screamed. That was illegal in this state and they could take my house and arrest me. Eye contact didn't stop her, so I turned to the now-anxious child to say that none of that was happening. The clerk burst into tears. "Oh honey, no! *You* didn't do anything wrong! No!" Time for a dramatic pause, but we were out of there.

Outside chances

Living can be a claustrophobic accrual of one direct hit after another. Contact can be a problem, especially at any sign of the downturn people are watching for. This year, the decadelong holiday mall brawls broke out in twelve different states, spreading fast in an Instagram of contagion. A dropped chair mistaken for a gunshot set off a stampede of people running over the tops of each other.

The word "change" now drifts by like a gas looking for places to solidify. This year, Trump dropped into the mix, like a fatty residue.

The weak links go off, and we're all weak links sometimes. I was walking my dog when a man screamed at me not to let her pee on his yard, which we had already passed uneventfully, but as I was fending him off with screams of my own, she peed in his neighbor's yard, triggering his full-throttle string of abuse popping on all cylinders. Another dog walker had paused twenty feet from me, standing there to witness. She said don't let him get your blood boiling, he's a nutcase; at least we use our doggie bags. She was trying to pull me back to the good; we were good enough and somehow together although a little cowed. His words were spitballs; hers were gently bouncing tennis balls. He was a rage machine; she was a sympathy machine, but she seemed so tired, too, and I could only imagine why.

The phrase "people are idiots" is the lingua franca of the moment and, OK, enough said, but there's also a lot of work going on here. Any pressure point is a social tendon tweaking. A shift in direction is a friction even if there's no disagreement. And then the social took a fall and suddenly other people became unbearable.

(WEAK LINKS; PRESSURE POINTS)

Writing Lessons

Twenty years ago I had an intro to cultural studies class right after a yoga class I was taking. I always fell asleep during the final relaxation, which disconnected me from my drivetrain, so I'd walk into my class and just stand there, looking around, for thirty seconds. That's a long time. The first time it happened, the students looked anxious, some aggressive, the room swelled. I said, "What's going on?" Then they started to smile at me, which surprised me, then we played a writing game to get started: What happens in the room when ... Make a list of what you worry about, what you're addicted to, the one hundred things you'd have in your tiny house if you could, why the old boots and not a paring knife?

Here's one to try: What influences have you been under? Where do you begin? Stress, marijuana, beer, rough transitions, other people's problems, animals, things you've read, women's night at the Rubaiyat, all the things that go on in academic committees, harmony singing, the twist of a relationship or fate, fictocriticism coming out of Australia, having money problems, watching loved people die, a first confession, age seven, when the priest asks, "Have you ever been impure . . . was it alone, or with others?"

Ten years ago all my classes became writing workshops. The price of admission is five hundred words. The writing can't be an exegesis of the reading; it has to have something to describe. Writing is a labor of being; it needs materials to work with. You have to start somewhere, you light on something, you lean into a realism of slippages and swells. Worlds are already so compositionally full that the question is not how to choose what to stay with but how to feel your way in.

In the workshop, anxieties have to be relieved; we have to learn that silence is OK waiting for a volunteer to read, or comments to start. We read four pieces in a row, the others finding ways to listen to write their own response compositions. Concepts become voiced improvisations working across threads; projects develop like sediment. The questions get really basic: what is it, what's it doing, where's it going, how do you know? The room gets collective, comedic, sharply intellectual, building habits of thought. It's a simple relief like pushing a restart button. It feels like a miracle, though.

Fish in Drag

Think about what you do when you revise a sentence, seeking a precision that gets at a situation so well that the empirical expands. You add something, delete something, substitute tenses; you rearrange clauses and phrases, remember another thing that happened that made this thing more of an event, and with each change the world offered to your readers shifts. Any attempt to delineate in words even the smallest moment— a greeting in the street, the opening of a window, the startling sound the world slips in—necessarily leaves out more than it includes, which is nothing to despair about.

(FISH 2012)

Suicidiation Nation

My spell-check says that any way to spell suicidiation is wrong. It *is* wrong that we walk into walls for life. That we type with broken wrists. That the soundtrack to the day is an engine scraping the last oil off its crevasses. That the small voice barely heard in the grinding will break itself to feel approximately free. That to appear healthy a gummed-up drive will surely reappear as desire.

Most of us are not crazy. Yet if we broadcast the rants that move through our heads while pausing at long red lights we'd be blown away by the police for conspiracy. How do we make a LEGO from a bundle of tirades? Or LINCOLN LOGS from them? Or twisted twigs from them of a paper so brittle it could fuel a fire? We are flinging ourselves at the encounter to catch its leakage with our mouths. If we blow it is not evidence that we were more broken than the other dangling modifiers and shattered loves. Each morning the existential question of breakfast allegorizes the being in life of the life-form of the day. Nothing is habitual or utopian enough to make the world-beat of attrition go away.

(REGAN 2017; SEDGWICK 1990)

The Morning Demons

We are all tired in a row, slouching in our humped coats. Mothers crouch to feed their children little spoons of yogurt. Adults read while digging out oatmeal from small cardboard boxes. A few people declare fuck it! and down a second donut. TSA cops jostle in garrulously. One of them asks if he can share a bit of the hand cream I've just pulled out. I grin with a thrust of fake chagrin and things seem easy for a second. It's easy to chat about dry air with strangers; harder to pretend that we'd all storyboard the same paradigm of order.

Near Midway Airport there's an enterprise zone pocked with donut shops selling Chinese food and bilingual nail salons. There is a factory, too, stashed away from the main drag, where most American donuts are baked and fictitiously distinguished by brand. In its cafeteria all the kids are skinny and the adults all fat except for the alcoholics, who are bone-dry and fierce in a way that would be desirable if their bodies seemed more energetic and fresh. My table neighbor wears a big flower shirt that looks like an egg's been broken on it by a heart-shaped rock.

A Place

I was a townie north of Boston. We had a loyalty to the expressivity of things. We knew when a few pansies stuck in a window box was a failed gesture, that a front porch cluttered or too bare was not just a bad sign but an actual slackening, as if the plastic siding, long ago layered over the wood, was itself necrotic. It was as if whatever there was to notice was already scored onto matter. We felt the bony truth in the mantra that the beach is cold and gray in the winter, and windy in a bad way. Our noses would swell and fill with blood if the heat was left on at night.

Sociality was a fleshy opening. We broke the ice with a smile or a swear word followed by a shrug, "What are ya gonna do?" We shared inconsequential things: a taste for Pecan Sandies, the habit of wearing sandals in the snow, eye contact around the Dunkin' Donuts, jaws slackening into town accents. We beached ourselves on down-to-earth voicings: "It is what it is." "That's enough of that." "No more beer for you." "No more talking to her." We put an end to cooking on the patio or music with dinner. When someone died, a thousand walked to the wake not because community was something stamped on us but to witness en masse the weight of the world.

Everything we did was a turning point ending in a quagmire. Mindfulness wasn't even a thing. Nothing ever happened without first registering a commitment to exhausting webs of complication, resource issues, and dark little tunnels of limited choice. It was as if the point was to spend ourselves in the effort of living.

We were agoraphobes drawn to an edge. The town line's patch of gray asphalt held the promise of sentience itself. Race, class, and ethnicity hovered above it as if the world had literally burst into color on the home side and gone gray in the instant of passing over the edge. And yet the town line had to be breached; it was a faltering onto a venturing out. We winged it, almost deliberately unprepared, driving with our heads straight ahead, as if we had no necks. Things happened when you set out to get pita bread from the Lebanese place one town over and only one mile away. Disorientation held promise.

No one knew street names, as if there were no circuit between the street signs our eyes must have seen and what we considered our business to know. I remember deliberately focusing on a street name to remember it, but that felt like the bleak loneliness of a solitary figure in an Edward Hopper painting.

Rules proliferated, sparking circuits of blame, guilt, rage, and humor. A trip to the recycling center meant knowing where to put newspaper, cardboard, glass (green, brown, clear, other), grades and sizes of plastic containers, types and weights of metals. Your trash should be clean. Nothing left on the pavement. The signs were confusing in their excess. Some people tried to follow the letter of the law, others swore loudly as if the rule makers could hear them. Some did a drive-by, shoving bags and boxes of unsorted trash out the sides of their cars and speeding off past the police station as if they could be chased down, not thinking yet of surveillance cameras.

Townies felt the pull of all the possibilities in a scene, what characters might do. We raised an eyebrow for emphasis. Bars had the hyperplain intimacy of a sixties basement rec room.

(A FEW PANSIES STUCK IN A WINDOW BOX; HOPPER; PITA BREAD; TOWNIES)

A Skeletal Thought

A paradigm is not a visible thing like a scaffold. It's the concept that any relation might become. To Agamben it creates and defines the intelligibility of the set to which it belongs. Maybe! Only if "defines" means "shapes." Yet intelligibility has nothing to do with the visible: it points to a sense that a thing has a shape that can be used as knowledge. In this paradigm of paradigms singularity and generality emerge like lovers from the same door. It's a field organized by tensions of difference that are not antitheses.

Write down all of the resonances the ordinary holds for you, its senses, practices, accidents, things. Set a timer: otherwise you'll never get to any other kind of exercise. Circle one and describe a scene until your language lapses.

I walked into the neighborhood mini-Target in search of underwear. It says a lot about your neighborhood when a mini-Target counts as gentrification. I asked a salesperson where the women's underwear was: I was looking for something rare and specific, but I didn't tell her that. In the world of erratic goods you can never be certain of what will be encountered. She said, "We don't have any women's underwear." Actually, what she said was, "No."

Me: "No?" I looked around. There was a rack of underwear for the manly in three-packs, from boxers to jockstraps. Me: "But look, here are men's underpants!" and, scanning, "some others marked for women!" Then in the blind spot behind my shoulder I saw a three-tiered rack stacked with lacy bikinis. "And look at these! Wait! Are you saying to me that I've aged out of these underpants?" She looks at me frankly. "Well, I *guess* you could still be working it." I laugh. "Most girls come here for something cute."

Waiting is waiting for composition to happen. Its place is not precisely location. It's a way of seeing composition and feeling the electricity without knowing where it comes from or having an intention. The surface of your thinking is cracked but reclaimable like a puzzle or a love letter torn up because one more thing is *too much,* or the alien sound you fear but then forget about when it stops repeating. The banality that becomes too-muchness in a snap when you can't extract enough air from the world can become a resource when at some point the lapse starts to matter.

(AGAMBEN 2009; BARRY 2008; FORRESTER 2007; MAYER N.D.)

Utopian Capitalism

Most people I know think Disney World is a grim joke they don't even want to hear. Fans, on the other hand, are all the way in. You can spot the master sergeants in the crowds: sharp-eyed women of a certain age reporting their campaign of the day from the primo chaise lounges they scored for the fireworks.

For me, Disney started as an online planning addiction driven by fear of heat and crowds and fanned by the usual pitfalls. But Disney's web support turned out to be a hospitable high-functioning shoot and the World itself was capitalism polished to an animatronic sparkle with MagicBands, FastPass+ lanes, highly competent hospitality majors working check-in as cast members.

Everyone says Disney is an attention to the perfect detail. Composition all the way down with no reveal. The princesses at the photo-op stations never break character--they're poised, kind, always white, unwinking. Photographers pose the little girls with one hand bent out from the wrist, as if this was the way it was done in some elsewhere. Cast members' roles are a closed-circuit division of labor in uniform: train conductors, shoppe-keepers, barbers, hatmakers, glassblowers, candymakers. Guests stay in the heady icon lands of the Yellowstone geyser, the Adirondack lodge, the riverboat-bayou settlement, the Great Gatsby golf course and jaunty outfits, the tropical paradise, the urban palace to the contemporary, the music/styles/cars/dances/tastes/lingo/living rooms of pop culture writ large. An aesthetic of the add-on winks at form's completion: women and girls don Minnie Mouse ears with bows and trailing veils, candy apples have Mickey Mouse ears, rooms have Little Mermaid canopies and patios for the Magic Kingdom fireworks. Fantasy Land celebrates the "as if" of the once was. Epcot revels in the anecdotal accomplishments of the Anthropocene: this cheese was France; these cowrie shells were Africa; these meatballs and fish were Norway. Ecological research produces a lemon tree with nine-pound lemons. Knowledge is a side effect of forms performed. It catches the eye like a Goofy character pop-up. That's what makes Disney cutting-edge.

A week in the World licenses a perceptual machinery already in full swing in the built environment it helped inspire; you might feel it in the breakfast room at your inn in Philly, or even in a scene of construction workers having lunch on a stoop on a city street, or in Little Italy, or a wig shop.

(ANIMATRONIC SPARKLE; MAGICBANDS)

Chicago

A place in Chicago looks like Amsterdam, clean-aired as though it has always just rained, with seating areas covered so the river can be enjoyed. On the water, bags and boats float. White rock music from the year of my divorce echoes in the dark and light greenness of everything under the gray sky. It feels like a favorite color has been achieved. Workers smoke here. Lapping noises and a breeze too cool for summer make the rust on the nearby warehouse seem OK. Writing outside in the extended adolescence of an undecided dusk seems OK. The ducks swim nonchalant.

(

I sat down a few decades ago, and when I got up there was a buttmark on the couch, a face with no nose to hook into the crack to keep me fixed. Nothing holds me here but the history of my attempt to be held, it turns out, and even that's over as fast as a snap, a harsh or a simple look. Attachment's like a book on the bookstore sidewalk that now in the middle of a humid summer feels coarse and bendy, worth not even a dollar.

So I sit down again to write. The mark of history on my back turns my front to the wind, like Adorno said. He's on my mind this morning, writing a wrecked world back into endurable form. He's on my mind this morning, waiting in a lonely place for his collaborator, without whom there's only loose scrolling through a life built carefully just beyond the nose. A friend with a 'fro and aviators waves at me on the lake, his young son scrolling nearby on a scooter. The friendship has turned out to be slight. The kid looks away and awry, confident of love.

Other people's confidence excites me. On a summer day in the early morning the lakeside is full of it, a sense of pride that we all show up for movement that no one pays us for, like trivia games at the ballpark or the energetic dinner-table debates that don't matter. Some people are snobs about their small knowledge and lord it, but I'm a dog with a sock.

Those pleasures are free and the fighting is play, all winking takes and soft pauses relieved from the usual pushy wish for importance that we try to hide from the radar that judges us for ridiculous desire.

(ADORNO [1974] 1991)

A return

I have a dream of going back. There's a shallow river where there was once a deep canyon and above that, rolling ranges of blue mountains. A dozen people of all shapes and sizes are climbing up on each other's shoulders like cheerleaders getting into a triangle formation. The guy in the middle holds a towrope behind a speedboat. They take off. A heavy, older, blond woman falls off the top of the triangle and does a perfect landing in only six inches of water. Some kind of reckless flourishing in a carnival of ruin.

Then I'm visiting the place. The trees have grown up, obscuring the view. There's no trash pickup, so every day I find a place to dump a bag: at the boardwalk, outside the supermarket where the cashiers take their cigarette breaks, at a rest area, a restaurant. I have to case out each place, then get in and get out quick, a victory, a guilty fear. The signs on every trash can and dumpster threaten that violators will be prosecuted. But no local would pay for trash disposal.

I'm bossier in my New England—"Hey! Where's the exit? . . . What's going on with the restrooms? . . . How do you get this in here?" I'm talking again about cockroaches and the horror of a heat wave. I feel my sister Peg's visceral objection to turning on the air conditioner because there's a window cracked open upstairs next to her bed. I remember I need fresh air to sleep. I remember that toasters have to be unplugged when you leave the house. I see the outline of laughable topics that lead from the gut.

On the island, Peg and Pete shove grocery bags into the back of their pants when they walk the dogs in the marsh. Pete perks up when I tell him that Ronn buys doggie bags. "What? How much does he pay for them?" I don't know, three dollars, there's a law against plastic bags in Austin. "Well, ya," Pete says, "Duh! It's only a matter of time here, too, but that's why I get them to double bag at the supermarket." Pete is serious, but he takes my giggling in stride. It's fun to tweak a regional nerve, but I'm starting to want to branch out on my own.

At the hotel, an egg-cooking machine is driving me crazy. There's one dial for temperature and another for time. You lower your eggs into one of two baskets of steaming water. I keep opening still-raw eggs and throwing them away with loud sound effects. Others are getting upset that their eggs are getting mixed up. Finally I notice that there's a huge sign with detailed operating instructions, but we've all had enough of this, poised between a fuck-you shrug and an eye roll.

There's been a brawl on the Island. Some drunk young Asian American women met two drunk young Irish American women in the street who were crying because their dogs were missing. The Irish accused the Asians of eating the dogs (though they later claimed in print that they had said "beating" the dogs). There was a fight, a broken leg, some ribs, assumptions of victims and villains, money raised for medical bills but only on one side. Then they were all charged with assault and battery. Peg and Pete's take on it was that the only cop on the island might have been a weak link in the story. He's a character, a dress-up cop who likes to strut; they say he probably had no idea what to do with all *this*.

(AN EGG-COOKING MACHINE; A FUCK-YOU SHRUG)

Stony Island Story Problems

It's the first day of summer and everyone's scurrying to a thing they're unsure of, eyes locked away from the guy who's approaching the driver's side window. Jack the five-year-old rides by on his orange bike with propellers spinning a story about monsters, and nurses speed-walk debating how and how quickly to kill pain and men. A girl plays with a doll whose clicking eyeballs tilt back, bending over it like a Gumby. The mood's like trolling a building looking for a room where you're expected for an interview and as your confidence drains slowly away, a door opens unexpectedly.

Today I spent my entire month's pay on taxes, pet insurance, home insurance, and car insurance while the cat named Puck groomed himself on a chair I curb-snatched in the nineties. Then I went to the store and bought $50 worth of trash bags, dental floss, apples, vanilla, soup, and saltines. I was on my way to see a sick friend with the two pints of chicken soup and the box of saltines. He makes $28,000 a year and DebtBuster is helping him pay $5,000 in parking tickets. Getting to him means passing the new Dollar Tree on South Stony Island Avenue in the warehouse that used to be called Moo & Oink. Bug-eyed pig and cow caricatures used to cheer up the drive down there, but no more. Everything at the Dollar Tree is manufactured with poison, then dispersed through middlemen to the people who scrape. Out front we stand slurping our juice boxes and smoothies making sexlike noises because, you know, at the end of the day, it's all about the drive to be aroused without too much memory. And living on together, which is its own work. He has two small dogs. One of them's named Duchess.

(ŽIŽEK 2004)

Last summer

Last summer, sensory paraphernalia bloomed like algae. Ecological collapse shag-carpeted the earth with nature's corpse and a thick sheen of romanticism for the loss. Melodramas of mixed ontological status hit swells of feeling and the force of things colliding. Austin's extreme El Niño replaced its end-stage drought with two months of bad, bad rain. People in vacation cabins were washed downriver on a lethal ten-mile ride. In North Carolina, sharks bit off nine teenagers' limbs over two weeks. Then they were gone. One kid punched his shark, remembering that's what you should do, but then the shark took his other arm. There were attacks on Cape Cod, too—something going on with the Atlantic.

By the end of the school year, loud noises in the house made me jump. Some kind of traffic-work-parenting PTSD spiraled out of overstretched attentions; others were starting to talk about this, too, but it didn't yet have a name. And now, in the traffic-free north woods, I'm afraid of hitting wild animals on the road because signs warn, "Brake for moose or it could be the last time you don't." And in the lake, the light green water and sandy bottom give way to darkness, weeds catch at your ankles, the waves pick up, the bite of the spawning pickerel can draw blood.

Tennis lessons are twenty humiliations an hour. A flashback to childhood softball. Our teacher apologizes for his toss every time one of us misses the ball. The new woman cuts a hard eye at her son complaining about his job at the movie theater. The mother of five throws me some eye contact. Her husband says, "Come on, Katie, let's smoke 'em," and gives me a tip on my serve. He catches me in the library—"See you soon!" My right shin is so swollen I can't take stairs; this could go either way—permanent damage or a new core strength.

All summer, there were perfect wedding scenes in brilliant color poised like concept scenes on display: bridesmaids in yellow and lavender floating down to the harbor along the brick sidewalk, a bride standing in her white dress and veil on a rain-darkened wooden train platform at the edge of the lake, the groomsmen waiting at a distance, clumped in black formality against beds of geraniums and impatiens planted in half barrels. A pause in the mode of a pose. The seizure of a starting point, the dream of a perfect ending.

Wednesday nights the town orchestra played in the bandstand. People sat in lawn chairs on the grass, the scene surreally sharp, almost parodic, but with a light touch like a *New Yorker* cover or a Maxfield Parrish painting. Clumps of teenage boys swarmed the fields at dusk in types: responsible-young-men-in-the-making in chinos and golf shirts, bad boys in hoodies and sunglasses swinging their hips as they walked, comic-loving pairs and trios talking excitedly about their favorites. Across the green at the library, Try It Out Bags include everything you need to get started hiking, sewing, fly tying, candy-making, painting, knitting, being grandparents, reporting your own abuse, or saving energy. A flyer says, "You're Not Alone"; inside there are calmly detailed descriptions of your options in various bad situations, as if getting out of the bad just takes a little skill or a helping hand.

This summer something else was going on. At the town beach a gang of middle school boys on the raft chanted "white power" three times before the lifeguard kicked them out and Parks and Recreation had to call a town meeting to start a youth sensitivity-training program.

(PARRISH; TRY IT OUT BAGS; WAINWRIGHT 1973)

Let's Not Ask for the Moon

The summer's sloping humidity loosened an avalanche of au revoirs.

My neighbor's the father of two boys and two girls, and as he left them at camp one day they all stood still in the sun so beautifully, paper dolls. He waves, they wave, he stops, they pause.

Later at the airport a girl with ironed hair drags a new black carry-on to the gate. She's wilting. She just tried to adorable her way into a job and play-by-plays it noisily into a phone. Then she slumps down near her charger wailing, "Oh Jerry, Jerry, you tell me this *now?*"

(KOZLOFF 1989; PROUTY 1941; WEEKS 2011)

Minds at Work

It had been a week since the tropical storm hit the island and we were still waiting for things to calm. The hard muscle of the ocean threw tides up to the edge of the dunes; the sky spasmed; the waves were a solid line of breakers. The pelicans were returning but the sanderlings were still running back and forth in the yards as if they were running in and out of the surf. The intracoastal waterway was a solid brown; there would be no clamming until the saline levels rose.

The pillows had given me a neck headache. In the gray light of a post-storm morning, their plastic covers lay exposed, like the skin of a beached jellyfish. The sheets were sticky and damp with humidity; my toes retracted from the marshy carpeting. A wild wind beat the house from one side and then another, momentarily chaotic. The sky over the ocean was blotchy black and green like bruises on fat. I threw open the bank of windows to blow out the oppressive atmosphere, but the air in the room just swelled asthmatically.

There was a message from Fran's daughter, Mimi. I called her back. She had a singer's voice. We talked in the details and tones of a conspiratorial co-competence. This might be the last time the old lovebirds spend any real time together. Pop is frail, his senses shrinking in; Fran has lost her mind—"You think, OK, she's like a twelve-year-old, but really she's five."
"Oh. You'd never know."
"Yes, her social skills are beautiful."
I hang up. I try to wrap my mind around this. Fran is five now? So, then what? No more leaving them alone? No. I don't think Mimi has children.

We had been coming to the beach with Pop and Fran for a few years. They'd met again at eighty-five, after dating young, then separated for sixty-five years of marriages and kids, places, work, churches, and deaths.

Fran and I didn't have much small talk. We'd smile in passing or, left to ourselves, drop fast to the straight, harsh talk that men were babies, more work than the four kids combined and mean, cheaters—the whole thing. She had married her husband because they both loved to dance. Now she remembered loving her daddy: he was a Presbyterian minister; she followed him everywhere he went; every night after dinner he'd make a different kind of ice cream with them; every kind worked except the watermelon. The neighborhood kids would peek around the corner of the porch to see if it was ready yet.

This year she brought me catalogs to give to my mother so she could order her clothes online. She doesn't remember she died.

The next year we'd up the ante to two weeks together. But Pop would be too sick to sit on the swing on the porch holding hands with Fran. She would wander the house wondering what she could do to get back to the love.

Everyday Life in Early Spring

Butterflies and bees are on the way and rabbits pop out of their holes to unnerve us with their rapid-fire blinking. Fantasy stains the approaching air like the eddy of a fuck-you said out of love, so warm you don't savor it: it savors you. This genre of the world jolt makes episodes possible. Meanwhile, I whisper, "Life's a racket," to the playground kids lolling all nutsy and tilt-headed, but why? Their loose play's about to lose out to this sharp tongue, that police tape, this dirty wash, that bad listener, and the daily perp walk to work, that's why.

Atmospheric Pressures

Belize blues is a muscular abandonment, an atmospheric pressure brooding, a paradise dream sagging like fallen haunches. No community of happy locals unfolds to swallow up the expats, who say they would have tried to help. Like a seesaw, a bloated reverie of magical transport drops into a land of "nothing but" thieves and drug addicts.

On the mainland everything waits and drifts. People sit on stoops by the muddy, heavily rutted road. Trucks drive by at a walking pace. The Mennonites make what machinery they need for their farms and the rice factory. The scientists hang out in their barns watching them invent an apparatus to study how sound travels through Mayan mounds in a rain forest.

The Cayes have a constant sea breeze. Ganja time meets the white, ironed blouses of the tourist industry in the constant repetition of intimate informality: "OK guys, thanks guys, see you later guys." The graffiti spells "poor gang." Up island, grandiose resorts rise out of a wasteland of scrubby fields and piles of construction debris. The Guatemalans sell their weavings on the beach. The Kriols sell mahogany carvings of sharks and rays, showing their sanded-down index fingers to prove they're the carvers.

(LITTLE 2012)

After Meth

After the email from the public library I throw his duffel bag in the back of the car. It's overstuffed with cans of fruit salad, sardines in oil, and the books I'd been desperately searching for. He smells like tin and dirty wool. He's disheveled and unfocused. He asks to be taken to a drugstore for lunch. "My body runs on energy drinks. Every city has its own ecology."

Each morning he showers for an hour and the house fills with a scrubbing sound so incessant you can imagine only harm being done. We go through fifteen bars of soap in a month. "The government sees everything and I can walk anywhere and feel the CCTV. It reports to the center where secrets are sifted. *Mon professeur!* Procure me some refreshments if you will, including canned fruit. I'll need them cold enough to hold me through my next assignment."

A black cat walks outside this café every few hours to sit under the cars. I want it to be social; that's its way of being social. It makes a gang sign with its paw, I swear, when it stops to do a little grooming. Then it walks back into the bicycle store and my screen goes blank suddenly because I forgot to continue typing while absorbed in his absorption.

When we met he brought a friend to check me out, a college roommate from back in the day. He said, "I looked you up, and I'll have YOU know I'M the original feminist!" Then he insulted my tight smile, which I deserved. What does it mean that the heart draws broken metal to its dump? Now I'm forced to leave the room whenever I hear, "Each time it's different but what's the same is how moved I am every time."

(BAUDELAIRE 1857; JACKSON 2005; WELTY 1994)

Thought practices

Write the sentence "Matter has a heartbeat" and let it be a guide for re-thinking thought's air supply.

Make a word balloon for the social atmosphere of a smell or a texture, or the way a shoulder twitched. Then conjure its world.

The artist Nina Katchadourian experimented with repairing torn spiderwebs with red thread and tiny tweezers. Then, finding the threads on the ground the next day, she made it her practice to film the spiders surgically excising the threads from their webs and then re-repairing them.

What's the thought practice for what seems incomprehensible but then makes perfect sense?

(A SHOULDER TWITCHED; KATCHADOURIAN 1998)

Approaching the Commercial Corridor

As I lock my car a priest in black robes walks onto a balcony across the street in this neighborhood of three flats and dormer houses, the balconies actually glorified fire escapes. The priest carries an armful of gorgeous flowers. On the first floor beneath him a tall bald woman pokes her head out and sees the effects of the cause I see, the priest throwing the red and yellow and all the greenery over the balcony edge like a water balloon or concrete mass intended only to hurt someone. She looks up at the floor he's standing on and I stand to the side also seeing him trying to get away with something, maybe wishing he could keep his back to the world whatever direction he turns.

The house next door has a big yellow chick taped to its front window hailing Easter. The house next door to that hasn't picked up its mail in a while. The house next door to that has a little white barking dog living it up in the submerged alley. A few doors down the air smells like oregano and burned cheese, and across from that a beauty parlor offers threading and weaving.

What the houses are doing

Every day I take a walk to check out the new neighborhood poised on the lake edge. At first the houses are disheveled, bruised, their yards are woodpiles, axes, chain saws, coolers, pickups, campers, boats, a fire pit, a shed. I know from the Zillow app that there's green carpeting inside and that an aesthetic aimed at filling in the empty spaces overwhelmed itself, decorations covering the cheap walls, baskets cramming the tops of the kitchen cabinets. A bareness tips into the almost hoarding of inadequate closets. The effect is the split realism of an aesthetic half realized and half succumbed to.

Piles of plastic boxes in a corner of the living room or spilling out over the couch onto the floor litter the living with something not right. As if things can't stand up anymore. Painfully steep stairs lead to tiny bedrooms painted bright colors in flat paint. There's nothing in the rooms but dark furniture. Or again the collapsed piles that started by the windows. The online photos are smudged, dark, some sideways or upside down, presenting the house as a horror to look away from. I guess there was no money for professional photographs, but what happened next?

Down the road, the houses on the lake are artful tunnels of viewing pleasure; the glass front door frames a route through gleaming surfaces to the blue lake and the purple mountains on the other side. The yards are a crafted spread of pine-needle beds and daylilies in clumps.

My walk ends at a sandy dead end circled by old camp houses from the fifties. They have rope swings hanging out over the lake, their upstairs windows are tiny, and there are all-weather chairs in the yards.

(SEIGWORTH 1998; SELF-DEFEATING DIY HOUSE-FOR-SALE PHOTOGRAPHS)

On Editing

Our editing discipline involves decisions, mostly as given, like the hundred-word unit. But still there are other overs and unders, punctuation exerting writerly will and unexpected contraction too: and spreading. We ask our readers to perform the jamb when language overruns the mental breathing that reading leans on. We cannot know for whom the text will become a riot, a notice, a wormhole, or mote. We prompt attention with an extra phrase or a subsentence here and there. The point is to jolt the eye amid the flow of things that will turn out to have detours, despite the editing.

This Week in Shakes

The protein drink is a chalky substance diluted and well-enough flavored that a small store sample persuades you that you'd drink it at home—only to find at home that, no matter how much attention you'd paid at the time, you can't get the makeup to look as good or the hair to fall again the way it did at the original moment of optimism. I had committed to two tubs of vegan breakfast powder. One recalled inhaled bugs and the other a bully shoving my face down hard into tough wet dirt.

When it comes to experiments I commit my mouth. Five months of persistently pasty tongue prison let out finally and I leaped to acquire seven new shake packs full of promise and percentages. Today: Vega One all-in-one nutritional shake in French Vanilla: "50% of daily intake vitamins & minerals, 15 grams of protein, 6 grams of fiber & 1.5 grams of omega 3, plus antioxidants, probiotics and greens. Dairy, gluten & soy free, no sugar added, and 135 calories. Complete daily essentials to help you thrive. Good for your body and the planet: clean . . . without compromise." The ampersand's shortcut efficiency figures negativity baroquely.

My shake was green. The world has not enough water for everyone, nor amounts sufficient to dilute this shake so that its flavor could be rejoined at the party after the chaos of getting in, finding the room with the coats, and moving outside for a quick smoke. Vanilla is a tart baby when you drink it from the bottle and a teasing allusion if you bite the bark. Vanilla is also the sex you slide into, the pleasant event of that hand again there, or the feeling of feet arching. My tongue sought it out but never alighted.

TUESDAY

The dread of another virtue breakfast was superseded by politics, a painful twist of need and interest and vigilant bad reading. There was an online Punch and Judy show with all the thrill and erotic boredom of your average stalker rom-com. When fools fuck up, one faction calls the other retro, a mole, a vampire, a baby. A mob of tweeting lurkers converges on every speculative heart.

The mix of disgust and love keeps me quiet. The chocolate version of yesterday's mud was eleven additional calories, which will be chastised for my own good at the gym.

WEDNESDAY

Last night was spent battling the cat's episodic loneliness and so this exhausted morning's Vega Energizing Smoothie was an especially dreadful prospect, reminding me that the verb "to stomach" shows that bodies have not only their own ideas but also radically autonomous sovereign tongues. Vanilla Almondilla offers as its main gift what it doesn't have: dairy, gluten & soy free, no sugar added. In the Coke Zero era a food's ideal contribution is its subtraction of dark consequences from the pleasures. 90 calories, 10 grams of protein. Xanthan gum is the aspartame of the health shake, which is also green.

THURSDAY

The iPad reads aloud in the kitchen this morning while I pull things together. Voice Dream offers a woman's halting, phonetic literalism to relay a scholarly book on comedy that prefers spectacle's excesses to narrative's enchainment. My naked partner enters the white room holding the ginger cat. He wonders, is it the Russian model of narrative where y is the effect of x or the Aristotelian one of intensities, reversals, and consequences? Raw Protein Beyond Organic Protein Formula features Bob Marley brand coffee: it is free of gluten, dairy, soy, fillers, artificial flavors, and good ones. I can't stop laughing.

FRIDAY

I spent the last night alone and so the morning was like a hotel morning with its shapeless offer of waking without obligation to be a particular way. The noise of a mind open to a limited formlessness makes breathing and blinking worth nothing in particular, and I considered taking a break from breakfast altogether because of the quiet. But the night's move through finitude required some pause after I lifted my head up and laughed at how turtle that everyday stretching is. I say to myself get ahold of yourself. The Vega Energizing Tropical Smoothie was wonderful, a wonder.

SATURDAY

I'm well acquainted with the genre of the Skype dinner date with old lovers. After recipe hunting left me numb, today's shake was my dinner protein, Vega Reparative in Berry—a revoltingly sweet attempt at Nestlé Quick Strawberry. I reenacted to my love a scene from *Domestic Violence* of an old white woman telling stories on her husband, a college professor who'd so abused her that she saw an angel flying around her room looking down kindly to offer advice from the high white ceiling. "I know I'm crazy," she says softly, with her rice-paper skin like mica, awry.

SUNDAY

The woman with Parkinson's swims every day and on each seems to diminish a little, which I sense because she always wears the same pants, of a slightly burnt orange hue. Bending stretches things out, so don't presuppose, I tell myself, knowing too that in the future a snapshot of this naked tableau might well portray a situation no one could have known. We used to talk about her bad back, which we now have nostalgia for. She laughs at my Amazing Meals shake, with its grainy austerity. I dash it down as though I'm late for a very important date.

(GERONIMI, JACKSON, AND LUSKE 1951; GILLESPIE AND COOTS 1938; WISEMAN 2001; ŽIŽEK 2004)

Lifelines in the middle of nowhere

We broke down in the middle of nowhere, south Texas. No motels, no rental cars, just flatlands and vultures, pickups and semis carrying gas and oil. I coasted into a dirt parking lot at a crossroad, across a sand and asphalt expanse from the Gillett General Store and the Hole Café.

I had barely thrown up the hood when a woman pulled up in a late-model pickup and turned off the engine, grinning, holding eye contact. Do you need help? Her wedding rings flashed, her nails flickered neon colors and gems as her fingers swiped her phone and iPad. She was working me out of the bad. She knew a guy with a shop up the road a ways, or a mobile mechanic could come, what's it doing? She got them both on the phone, "Roberto, qué tal, hay una familia aquí . . ." She switched into the laughable by way of an ending. "Well, that's life. They say your house and your car are your worst investments!" She let that settle on the scene before she pulled out.

Pickups stopped every ten minutes. "Do you need help? That's the way it is, it's always in the middle of nowhere." "It didn't *look* like a repo." "We have all our food." "Yeah, every year we have to go to Sam's Club even though we end up at the supermarket in Corpus every day anyway. Then we carry boxes of food home when the grandkids leave. It's never simple." "No. What do people do around here?" "Oil rigs, prisons." "The detention centers?" "Yup." "What's that like?" "Shitty." "Yeah."

The mechanic said it was bad and a holiday, parts would have to come from San Antonio and it was a turbo. He was from Ohio, which was backward, originally West Virginia, backward too, but nothing like Pennsylvania. The Pennies were mean. He moved to Texas because he got tired of the cold. I asked him what I owed him. He said twenty. I gave him forty because he'd told me a story about buying a gas can and taking twenty dollars of gas to a woman out on the highway. She said how much do I owe you and he said fifty. She gave him a credit card but it didn't work so she said well here's twenty, I'll put twenty in gas in your truck. "Mmm-hmm."

I had to pee. The store was just closing, a woman came out waving me back as I was crossing the street: "Estamos cerrado. No venga, no venga." "OK," turning around, but then one of the men sitting in the car waiting to pick her up got out and waved me back "Solamente necesita ir al baño. Ayúdela."

Two hours later, the tow truck arrived. The driver asked me twice if I wanted him to call someone to come sit with us. "No, friends are coming." We stood in the dirt with our suitcases, computer bags, coolers of food, pillows, a fishing rod, a guitar.

Hefty with Febreze

The rusty sound of a door hinge opening and a latch decoupling opens the dream, which is set in a dark forest. I drag a heavy trash bag walking backwards. I reach a hut and pull the bag in, then puke into the bag for a very long time. For a dark while you see my bent body and where a head would be, the bag. Grating retching noise predominates, uneven and unpredictable. I hoist the dead into the dumpster and use my sleeve to wipe my mouth. Because there is no full access to my face it is hard to tell whether I'm evil, good, anxious, or grim. All you know is that I'm focused.

It would be wrong to say that the violence took place offscreen, but no more wrong than to say, "Well, I turned out alright," as though a good end vindicates the violence or justifies the scar tissue called personality if one appears interesting and complex. Hypervigilance isn't intelligence either, even if it's highly cultivated. Achievements produce defenses against their own openings. Events give you something to talk about, passing time. What is a film loop evidence of? Idealizations come and go. Genre's a blanky.

(LYOTARD 2004)

A Family Line

I remember the night my mother left, running across the fields through lightning and heavy rain to the big house burning. It had ten bedrooms. The fire was so hot it melted the silver on the dining room credenza. The house had Irish linen brought from County Cork; they said there must have been money. Aunt Irene was still living there, the smell of smoke saturating her skin, a bad smell.

Once another aunt let slip the detail of the "funny cigarettes" men would bring to the big house. There were town Easter egg hunts on its pond, then the pond was on a triangle of land wedged between busy roads, and then it was a trashy, barely wet spot behind a strip mall, and then high grasses grew and blew in the wind.

The family was a hard ecology. They called it alcoholism, the brothers fighting with fists and knives, the sisters and wives driving them off with a milk bottle to the head, a sturdy board kept under the bed. Hard, competent women ineligible for downtime, men with laboring skills and monkeys on their backs, the children sent out to pick potatoes for dinner, don't tell anyone that's all we have to eat. Resilience and faltering remembered in the stories of the ends people came to. Uncle Jack killed young walking home drunk one night, Uncle Billy in his narrow bed in a brick tenement, his smell dense with tobacco and old man things, a rich uncle's suicide in the wake of a political scandal, the stain my mother felt in her blood when things were bad in the end. She and her sisters built a world like a skin around horrors backed away from like the workhorses they hated. Massive haunches were a topic. Penises never were.

In the Terminal

Shy children weave around the space waiting to get taken up by something and dreading it too, and I mean children in the religious sense I don't have to paint for you, who bend so slow and queer from the hope a touch can be a link. I don't need to paint it for you, or to be honest I write but keep erasing because examples are what we bring to each other.

In the harsh airport light I ran into a friend I didn't recognize without his beard. It was like when you say, "My friend . . ." and their name escapes you suddenly, although you can see them, hear their voice, and remember things about them that carry the tone of who they are. It's humiliating when a friend appears in ellipsis; it exposes your love's brittle strings. I didn't know him white-skinned, puffy-fresh; I could tell that I'm aging out of his image of me, so the belated smiles were OK. Between the wish to bomb unbearable schmucks and the desperate desire for loved ones to die their own way and stress and poiesis, we talked about suicide. The stories forged the closeness of inexhaustible things.

(AUGÉ [1992] 2009; BION 1959; DANIEL 2017; KLEIN AND RIVIERE 1964; LAYMON 2013; STOCKTON 2009; TAYLOR 2015)

Kinships

If you're nice to the people you want to love, smiling wide like a ventriloquist, probably no one will notice the labor and they'd be downcast if you didn't try. The first smile is usually a real something, and it glues you tightly to little worlds. The rest of the time is all free fall: drinking Coke, eating chips, chasing tail and stories, becoming strong-legged from scavenging more life too, a lonely giant in your wild mind. In the long run—but who lives in the long run now? The aboriginals, that's who. "Originals" move in obedient time to the ritual the law permits. May "the comfortable" be blessed by an afterlife in story problems teaching hard subtraction. May "the disturbed" forget the difference between being deserving and a felt need. For all of us consolation-sniffers, may our fall find bounce. Back in the day a whole world of people mouthed things to you out of love. You've carried everywhere the charcoal record of their clown-words so that sketches would unfailingly be there to play with; and so you can say you too have been loved in a world that has otherwise insisted it's up to you not to abandon it.

(for Beth Povinelli)

Intimacy needs a sign on the wall like UNBALANCED LOAD. One time Katie's skin turned black with a virus and then years later behind the knee it reappeared, not race black but the beef jerky black of a dead body patched onto her moist pasty one. It was a passive-aggressive haunting like all symptoms, waiting around to be noticed like an inconvenient child. A symptom is just one kind of concept in the world. It makes keeping track of reality impossible, and that makes people hysterical. In the era of the action item a symptom is just one more thing.

(for Katie Stewart)

Projects

A team of beautiful young women dressed like field ecologists built the new walkway and lined the front of the house with the cast-iron plant, rosemary, irises, and sage to hide the stucco. Then John worked in the heat to take off the weight gained from living on the street. He amended the soil in the garden beds with compost and sand. He was abusing his Adderall. I was a control freak. Once he made little mounds of pea gravel everywhere, like a Flintstones yard. I'd say where's the bucket I left for you; he'd say there never was a bucket, I have a teaspoon and sandpaper. I'd leave giant notes tacked to everything. One night I found a secret tunnel he was digging under the house. Later, I found a bachelor pad. He had lined the dirt with scraps of wood and dragged lights and extension cords and pieces of rugs down there. There was a place where he smoked, there were milk jugs full of pee. I found all this only when the termites attracted by the wood he had laid down reached such levels of infestation that they were flying into the house through the floorboards.

Friendhating

1. She is clueless and white: imagine a specific face and who would love that face. Her boyfriend is the same, warm through an aspic of sadness so sticky my heart turns toward and away from their Styrofoam kisses and weird hug angles. She is serious, but her language rings with "boo-boo" and "poo." She futures in adoration and exclamation points too. One day in a clearing on the edge of a wood they took me into their confidence. Before, it had been on a need-to-know basis, like most love. I learned then that the couple is a game of ricocheted glances and anxious head-nodding without clear margins.

2. She was standing in profile in the café doorway reading the wall. She was wearing grandmother beige and large plastic pearls of food-coloring colors. A self-induced haircut looked good from the front, with bangs and a slight framing wave. We said YES! to everything we could, which wasn't much, at first. Science shows that repetition produces facts. Enthusiasm can be the opposite of curiosity, though, even when you aim to do right by an object you think you know. In *The Case of the Grinning Cat* the philosopher litters the world with cartoon punims to help you catch up with what's happening. Other artists use semicolons to forge, or is it honor, or is it make, or is it insist on, or is it bargain with, or is it wink at, or is it operate on, connotations.

3. She wears perfume that kills all the bugs in her path, as though she is anti-fly. She is the kind of woman who stinks up the clothes she tries on in the department store and doesn't know it, or worse, thinks she is leaving a gift for the future woman the size four won't fit because it's too small, or is *not her*. But in the alcoholic mouth of a summer day, or around men, a glowy ball slowly lifts her a little above us, and there is real, genuine beauty.

4. I have loved me so many assholes. The one who loved calling other people stupid, the one who insulted secretaries, the ones

who puffed themselves up so big that the rest of us became minor characters, the ones who secured their charisma by shitting on lost and current beloveds, the ones who were so intentionally good there was no room to breathe, the others who blamed the world for their angst and every hiccup, the ones who thought they were all that and the opposite too, plus the ones I was related to.

5. Then there are the people, *my peeps*, who turn their faces to the world to say this and make that because what they see is what they have to give. I want to call their mode of being "The New Frankness" and share with them my future epitaph: "She did what she could do at the time." Once the state passed a law to help people who had babies they didn't want to keep. Any time in the first ninety days you can go somewhere and just leave the kid there, without having to pay or apologize or go to prison or be hated.

6. What's the difference between talk that pushes talk away and conversation?

7. I don't hate all my friends a little even a little. There's the tender one with dark black hair who is fighting to stay attached to things on the verge of dead. There's the person who calls us cartoon names and judges the funny-bad. There's the person who gets irritated if I get anxious. There's the one who is clueless that her face is a maniacal GIF. There's the Marxist candy eater. There's the one who is an amazing mother and you like watching her go at it. There's the one who is developing a sense of humor after a lifetime of devoted seriousness, and it's sweet to watch her loosen up and crack up. There's the one who is happy to see you. There's the one who likes, really likes, the way you think. Most people only kind of like, but when someone really likes, that's nice. There's the one who taught me the phrase "that's nice." There's the one

who jumps in hard and has to leave in an hour. There's the one who you respect so much your heart hurts. There's the one who has you in mind, then calls you up. There's the one who lifts your chin on contact. There is the one who just starts in without even so much as a hello. Then there are all the good conversationalists. Then there are all the grinners.

8. Eve Sedgwick's "White Glasses" is the best poem about friendship I've read. Foucault's "Friendship as a Way of Life" and Muñoz's and O'Hara's "Having a Coke with You" sit on that bench with her too.

9. There's a watercolor next to my desk, all red and purple like the horizon of a beautiful sunset, but with no sun. The clouds look like countries in the global south and the bottom is like the astonishing water outside Zadar that plays music when it hits the shore because someone there bore holes in the world to make even more beauty. In the middle there is a dark blue boyish man. He is wearing a backpack. His hair is tousled. His eyes are closed and he's a mouth breather. He is hunched over with his hands on his knees and his eyes are shut. He's outlined in black ink and filled with watercolors. Over him there's a motto painted in bile-colored letters: *You need exhaustion to think.* I like sensing the sight of the painting while I'm writing. The friend who painted it always gestures toward myth, believes in repair, doesn't care about the rational claim. It's like the world is his office and he's a therapist who is a little depressed at failing one more time but somebody's got to go there. He also painted a portrait of Freud in pink, blue, and brown watercolors. Freud's face is traced in wide brown strokes, as though with poo. But there is a pink and white aura around Freud in honor of his frank intentions, and a white-painted caption whose brushstrokes are visible in every letter. *We can't make you better. But we can wish you well.* It looks hastily done but not thoughtlessly. The caption cascades down the

front of the painting like the credits at the end of a film or the "one more thing" a friend blurts out when you're trying to get off the phone. It's the slightly inconvenient news that almost doesn't get said.

10. My old friend's face is turning square like a TV from the fifties. His companion animal is named Juicebox, a dirty white poodle wrapped in a red coat with official writing on it. My friend walks the world in pajama bottoms. He is not white, though. Talk's quietest tones pervade all the rooms he speaks in, because Juicebox is curled up sleeping in my friend's lap or the crook of his arm, and disturbing *that* won't decrease the world's vast shittiness. It's as though he were a guard hired to protect a painting from getting made into something else. You can't tell from that description how our friendship works, that we're relying on an indestructible substance that allows for tone to snap and risk exhausting the elastic. Comedy, pets, self-medication, and shared hates play with the scale of life across the madness and languor of being historical. He takes naps. I love that. He can because all his objects remain in the air whether or not he is awake.

11. Genre is a hopscotch grid drawn in the dirt that smears and fades its substance through use. My friend's face, as I was saying, is getting broad, its beauty extended diffusely like a person's in early dementia. A person with nothing you could call a margin; little you could call a cushion. He wishes the old technologies still worked. Because the grain of the voice forces messier contact than machine connection? Or because it's getting harder to trust in sync? When we meet our shoulders hook up as though we're toys on a grid and then it feels like a superhero team is responding confidently to an urgent call.

(BERARDI 2012; CAHILL 2014A, 2014B; FOUCAULT 1997; MARKER 2006; MUÑOZ 2009; O'HARA [1960] 1995)

What Comes Through

These days, the surfaces of things probe the lines of phenomena throwing together, as in "When did tattooing your head become a thing?" Sociality is a query into what others are doing and know. "How'd you get into *that*?" "What *is* that?" Surprise flourishes now because of all the conspiracies and occluded zones, sure, but also because things hit at such a specific angle, already on the way to a precise formation. What's happening activates a noticing competency and maybe even an impulse to be in what you didn't even know existed until just now, or to stay out of it. You can be contaminated by a pause or a tic in your mood.

Objects come through as if from behind. In Ann Hamilton's ONEEVERYONE, she had hundreds of people stand behind a floor-to-ceiling manufactured membrane like a skin. They couldn't see through it but they could hear her voice telling them to touch it with their hands or a hip. Hamilton's photographs angle onto the possibilities of touch. Some are larger-than-life and harder-than-fact ceramic photo-sculptures on display in the lobby of the Dell Medical School in Austin. Others are small and ethereal, placed over a landline phone or on a side aisle on the way to a restroom. Others were printed on newsprint, faint and shadowy and accompanied by writing, distributed as a free newspaper. There was also a nine-hundred-page phone book of wordless images, also printed on newsprint and distributed freely.

The photographs remind me of the partial yet precise points of contact in everyday life that register like a blip in the course of things. Casual sightings of something a little off, or partial, or in the middle of itself, can prompt ordinary speculation. In the photographs behind the skin, a body part stands out while others hang back in an amorphous atmosphere. A head, featured, looks too big; a face looks like a paper-doll cutout. A cheekbone comes through fully freckled, but the woman's hands, buttoning a lab coat, look older, as if they had lived a different life. The body parts are wooden objects in proximity as in a primitivist painting: there is a head and a hand and a scarf, there is a village in the snow with a barn, and skaters on a pond, and trucks loaded with logs, and running dogs, and ducks, and winter clothes. Precisions sharpened against a backdrop of what's uncertain and off-center derealize the facile presumption of a whole. Instead, focus draws down onto the question of what's in a fingertip, a flower, a freckle.

You stare at the way hair cascades down a woman's back, every strand thick and straight, or white and curled. You notice the way an object draws into orbit with others. The hands carry a harmonica; they wear beautiful black nail polish; there's a tattoo. Under the skin of a wrist is a tender vein; a small bone protrudes just slightly. A shoulder leans into a shawl; dog tags wrap a neck. There is a blood pressure cuff, an eye patch, a hospital wristband; a sharp pink tie sets off a dark suit and a white, white shirt. In a series of captures, events of contact take place as color, shape, the gesture of an aspiration, a repetition of touch. Hands hesitate, or they venture out like emissaries. The eyes speculate. Reactions ring out like the chorus of a song. Here we are. This is it. The eyes are a little wide, the poke of a finger sharpens against the soft, blurred background, there is a dimple, an eyebrow raises, an elbow turns.

(FRECKLES; HAMILTON 2012)

Everyday, a Video Installation

There's exquisite Black Arts avant-garde music playing. The voice that's reading a poem in it makes the world seem thick and floatable despite what's there in front of our eyes. Someone is locked in the trunk of a car—it's an old car without an antikidnap latch in it—breathing in their own body air and choking while the world out here spectates in nonchalance. In this lifeboat movie the anxious specter delays mourning in case of rescue. Such suffering was no one's ambition when we were born, but there it is: something says wake up and pee, then go make life.

(ABRAMS 1968; CRAWFORD 2017; SIMON 2018)

Collecting

He collects things because they were free, or a deal; they sit around him like matters of pure potential. They're his muses. They gather in companionable clumps: fishing rods with reels, hooks and flies (dry and wet, poppers), lures (swim baits, plastic creatures, crank baits, spinners), weights (split shots, drop shots), jewelry-making beads, silver, wires, finishings, and tools (pliers with nylon jaws, goldsmith hammers, beading needles, flush cutters), leather-working needles and oils, a knife shaped like a half-moon, awls, stains and dyes, stamps, swivel knives, waxed linen thread, leather lace, conchos, buckles, rivets, snaps, guitars with their strings, song lists, capos and stands, knives with cases and sharpeners, fountain pens with their jars of ink and cleaning methods, acrylics and watercolors, rolls of canvas, flat brushes and round brushes, brushes small enough to put the pupil in a doll's eye or four inches wide, books everywhere, with their bookmarks, the reading lights that hook onto their covers or hang on the bed frame, magnifying lenses with lights and book stands so your hands are free.

He enjoys his routines of care and repair. He is compelled to read catalogs. Now he's taken an interest in boats, he's learning the vocabulary of sails and engines, finishes and knots and navigation. He files in his brain all the details of all these interests and other useful items like springs and cabinet hardware. There's some peace in this but it's prolific too. He develops favorite companies; he mail orders more things. He decides to build a racing bike, and every day more and bigger boxes start arriving. He needs a certain kind of screw he can't find. Much time is spent searching for things that are needed to get started. But there are always treasures discovered. An object sets off a line of thinking.

If we could pay attention to everything

I can't say how many walnuts I've forgotten, charred remains spoiling the pan's iron bottom. Salad peas also languished and puckered in the copper pot's low simmer while I walked in the blithe idiocy of next things and torque. But forgetting's only one kind of inattention, duct-taped shut in a relentless screaming. It would be great if the fossilized air in bubbles popped and spit out second chances. It would be great if the "oh nos" and "not agains" reappeared as parties. If we could pay attention to everything, there would be no comedy.

Everyone leans on her desk, everyone leans on his desk, the animal does a downward dog and he's a cat, ordinary things impede productivity, therapy, and citizenship. Sometimes failure is just bad. Not queer, better, redeemable, a profile in courage, delicious, or a genuine experiment. Some days you throw up your "why bother?" hands. But because pleasure might rest under any scratch off, hard stuff's no bedrock. I eat noodles made from yams that smell like fish yet have no flavor or nutrients. Spectacle has been made the soundtrack to legs moving under a blanket in the dark. Silhouettes emerge from my fingers typing there was no dream.

(BERGSON [1900] 1914)

What is it to be naked among men?

The lake is infused with alien fish and smugglers dumped into the water unseeable things and soon bacteria were taking massive shits there, sending to the way of decay our sloppily arranged infrastructures. We are fucked from building haywire on ecologies like that, choosing, choosing, barely chewing, confusing survival for desire. Inattentive when bored, eating while driving, singing in the car, fiddling absentmindedly with this or that, and refusing to let go, hoping the dying takes place later, or over there. Empires end like that, you know, dissolving slowly while grammars stand dry-eyed on the shore waving, grinning, and making up new ways to be inconvenient. Now the shore shocks, reappearing as the edge of a cliff, the ground washed out while the bright light shines blindingly, all yellow-spiked and hopeful. Imagine a cartoon of the monster fish under the sudden cliff and subtract the promise of immortality that makes cartoons comical.

Harder's not always the same thing as worse. In the chronicles of disappointing touch there's a lifetime of accommodation and the throat wedges, trying not to suffer from the wrong wants again. Against that wind, the question asks itself: what is it to be naked among men?

In a crisis people flail. If x is like this, we can treat x the way we treated this. The state wants people to die: not like the Shoah, like the slow deaths of slavery, not like blue-collar exhaustion, like the life loss in migration, not like the banality of meat but the unpeeling that's leather. The nots are randomly placed. So look at all the ways x is not like this. Will a sick analogy respond to treatment? What relation obtains between treatment and repair? And justice, let us not go there.

Just now, another analogy went bad. That is the story of this, and many stories. In other ones, an analogy goes good.

After disaster, more love. After disaster, more democracy. After disaster, there is no after but a newly congested tableau of the present that motivates people toward cushions. "What *is* it to be 'naked' among men?"

Foucault asks. The quotation marks force a hole in the world that sucks disparate moments into vulnerable copresence. What is it to be *naked* among men? The italics are a resource for rebooting resonance. What is it to be "naked," where are you just now? The literal, the figural, staying alive.

(FOUCAULT 1997; MILMAN 2016; RAFFLES 2002; SPAHR 2011)

Camera Worthy

I was raking leaves in the backyard when I heard honking and yelling on the street. Thinking one of our dogs or cats had gotten out, I ran through the gate to find neighbors standing in the street yelling back and forth. "What was that?" "We should call the police." "Did you get her license plate?" A woman walking a dog and pushing a stroller had to walk around a parked car into the street (no sidewalks). A car speeding up the street nearly hit her and then stopped to yell, "GET OUT OF THE ROAD!!!" A young couple walking down the other side of the street told us the driver was well known as "the crazy driver" and there were You-Tube clips of her doing this kind of thing. The police had been called, her license plate had been circulated on the neighborhood listserv. There was a pause. We looked at each other. The scene felt overfilled and rickety, ricocheting off isolation, vulnerability, snap judgment, the state of place, the status of community watch, the thinness of commonality. I wondered where that crazy driver lived and what it was like inside her house, and her life, and her car.

The Strange Situation: A Wedding Album

Any phrase can open up a space to walk around in, if *You are not alone* is the scent it carries, if the impression it makes stays in the air, if it does nothing but offer even the slightest sense of a link. Sometimes it makes gravity pull away, forcing an unbidden freedom; sometimes it taints what seems unencumbered from another angle. But as the cat on the bathroom floor welcomes the cool without being grateful to it, and the fly darts out the window you crack without sending a thank-you note, when a way out appears as a way in we'll tend to scramble toward it without aforethought.

No one documented the slapstick crash. Near the highway the hill was pitched so steep that the squirrels tumbled down from a vast misreading of how hard the dirt was packed. We clambered up on all fours and lost a shoe. Hitchhiking to the wedding ensued and the AAA saved us on the side of the road, swerving to the airport and wishing us the luck it turned out we needed.

What was off about it wasn't cinematic. We arrived and my eyes opened to a small cluster of bug-eyed people. It was as though I had drawn them from my palm like taffy, liberating them into life without the snapping sound of lost teeth. In a minute the crowded room buzzed harshly, each friend perhaps wondering why they continued to show up just in case. Everyone places secret bets at a wedding. The laughter is a goldmine of realness.

Genre's an efficiency, like identity. I am lucky to be a dreamer because a dreamer never stops being interested. People know when they haven't said enough, that's why they dream. Or that's not why they dream but why they continue loving.

(AINSWORTH ET AL. 1978; BION 1959)

All I know is

It takes a lot more than clarity to keep someone going; there's more at stake than just knowing. Certainty can be an expressivity mistake, willful bullshit, or an out-of-body experience like spotting a dog poop on the living room floor as you try to make your way to the coffeepot in the morning. In the middle of things, already improvising with already felts, things tweak the nerve between epistemology and ontology.

I knew people who died because they wouldn't go to a doctor. Because they knew there was something really wrong and they didn't want to know. They didn't want others to know. They didn't want a doctor talking to them that way. What do *they* know? So they made a method of secrecy. They kept it to themselves while the others watched their bodies, afraid to say anything *to* them. The others talked, of course, but not much and at a whisper; they worried, but intervention wasn't even an idea. It wouldn't work; it would make things worse, no one wanted to sacrifice themselves on the altar of helping that's taken as an invasion.

The everyday is a radical empiricism, a weird realism, where things are not examples of anything but a profusion of forms performing their capacities in a situation. On a walk in the suburbs, Dillard saw a mockingbird take a single step off a roof gutter into the air and "just a breath before he would have been dashed to the ground, he unfurled his wings with exact, deliberate care" and floated onto the grass. Heading out to cop, a heroin addict's neighborhood is like struggling through high grass but then, later, after, the place is a different real—full up, wistful, exactly right; he wouldn't want to be anywhere else or doing anything else.

(DILLARD 1975; HARMAN 2012; MCCORMACK 2013; ROBINSON 2009)

Written in a place that smells like chicken

I saw my heart today oh boy four monstrous wormholes linked by flapping gates. And though the news was rather sad I had to laugh at the flesh egg's large pores, which sight triggered a jump cut to my poor cat's heart suspended in the middle of a gray X-ray showing a mass they called foreign when they meant dangerous. My hand has its own memory of that heart and the beat left behind by all the anchoring loves. Even this cut of pulsating holes is sound finding figuration. Blood expels blue and returns tired red. It gets used without being used up, is what blood does while you are still lucky. My doctor tells me that she is fried by the flood of broken systems and mental illness that seems the right response to how life is now. What is healing when illness is reason and reason a style you are supposed to fake to maintain being useful, convenient, and familiar? Breathing room is a way of catching up to that; elbow room is what your thrashing affects try to make in the middle of the encounters that can never let you be secure about where the middle is.

(JAIN 2013; LENNON AND MCCARTNEY 1967)

Anxiety made a nest in her

At twelve, a man screamed at her for having the dog off leash. We made jokes about it. He's a crab face. Everybody else *likes* dogs. But she's not taking any more chances. No new situation is safe—not miniature golf, not the supermarket, not the shoe store where there might be a rule against walking in the shoes to see if they fit. She wants all the rules posted everywhere. She thinks we're rule breakers and we'll get her in trouble. She's on her own and trying to get oriented. My fear of her anxiety makes me snap at her. "Are you kidding me?" "Get a move on."

In Philly we got caught in a thunderstorm walking back to the hotel. She worried about getting her new henna tattoo wet and the lighting. She wanted to take a cab. But then we were running in the rain, screaming alarmed, excited, it could have gone either way. In the hotel, the elevator was broken. We were soaked. We had to walk up four flights of stairs. By the time we got back to the room she had cracked wide open; her mouth full of ice cream, she couldn't stop laughing.

Book Reviews

1. POLICE STATE

There's a map on the web that pops up a poem about the Chicagos dead from police interaction at each site of the year's "incidents." Chicago blackness is live like that: an old homeless woman took a joyous shit in the Walgreens parking lot on 55th the first day I was in the city. We all stood around for too long, stunned: it is hard to see someone smile and shit, it confuses the rescue ambition. In that same spot today I saw a totaled sedan that looked like a mangled shark. People were standing by murmuring. Two men hovered near each other parallel and silent. One of them was old, my age. The other one was even older, the old man's father. I should say they were whitish men, their skins splotched various shades of potato. Behind them was a nice dark blue BMW. It's not rare in Chicago to see someone lose their freedom, or to demonstrate a freedom they don't usually enjoy. But there are consequences in this city. My neighborhood is home to effects and remains. The father's father's through with driving. Each of us is a neighbor attending to life and to forms of dying.

(REGAN AND HOLMES 2016)

2. WHAT BELONGS TO YOU

In an unexpected meeting last week a man giggled at his drunken irrationality and adjusted his pants. There is nothing I love more than watching someone use their freedom. If there's a thing like freedom and you use it I will love a thing about you. I'll coast in awkward transit, family meals, and acrid sex to get next to a freedom. I'll fling myself at ordinary monsters if in the crevasse of the mistake I get next to a freedom. We bear each other hoping to breathe in each other's freedom.

This is what it means to be amazed.

(FOUCAULT 1997; GREENWELL 2016; ZERILLI 2005)

The Twins

They shine. One is a ballet dancer. Music ripples through the muscles on his shoulders and upper back, taking the shape of a humpback on a wave. Joe's shine is more desperate, more drugs and brain damage from an attack with a baseball bat. When he was eleven he would leave the house at night and go into the storm drains. One night he came back with chemical burns all over his forearms.

They're not quite dialed in; they had a rough start. They're looking for something, changing the subject, wandering, perking up, asking basic questions they need the answers to. Do you think a doctor would be good for me to marry? We dance really well together. Would it be good to try to get a job in a bar, maybe? Which one? Where is that? How much would it cost to get an apartment? How do you get electricity? Every few minutes they move in for a hug. A touch.

They've been together only once in the past ten years. A reunion at their adoptive mother's who kept the dancer but not the one with problems. They all snuck out late one night and hung out in the neighborhood smoking cigarettes. That got him disinherited because it's a smoke-free neighborhood; you can smoke on your property but not on the street. The neighbors stopped giving him yard work. He misses the yard work. His brother masturbated to his girlfriend's pictures. He had to tell her. She said make sure it never happens again. So he took her pictures off his computer. She was mad, but it was the only way. She broke it off. Today he's following my lead, trying to get things straight. He has a meeting for a job but he doesn't know where it is.

All the Desperate Calls Rolled into One

Each day begins glasses off and a quiet reading of the world's noise. The cats, the street already flowing with joggers and cars, sirens because I'm in a city and inside the hover of yesterday's knee-buckling encounters. I call Katie for a refresher course in dedramatizing the crazy. We banter and cackle, then she says: rather than saying "I'm hurt," say "I feel funny" and "What's up?" Rather than saying "I want *x* to change," say "What if we did *x*?" I've also heard "Feel ten in your heart, act seven in your movements." "Smile like an animal tracking prey." "Don't rush to breathe: just write."

Baldwin says, love the racist enemy too fearful to ditch his vicious innocence. Imitation is the something of something but it's also a way of learning, and I'd give anything to sound loving-sad like that instead of not understanding the burst of what comes out when I play the keyboard. Because I love no one when I'm writing there's an everything—it's like laughter, fierce and emotionless. Norms are spongy, absorbing a lot and smearing the encounter with grit. I say embrace the love you feel surging when you're taken up by your whatever weapon.

(BALDWIN [1963] 1992; BARTHES [2002] 2005; BERGSON [1900] 1914)

It's Structural

Every house we lived in had a thing we called "the built-in." A built-in is an infrastructure for everyday order slotted into a closet whose frame would have read, "This house is mine" if things had signs revealing their true function. My father's change jar sat there, a large brandy snifter that was once for something else, a terrarium or ceremonial candy. His watches lay there too, just next to his cufflinks. Near them were his stacked white laundered shirts, each of which had supportive cardboard in the back, and if you slid it out carefully you would have a thing to draw on. Today I emptied mine, for $27.23. His was full of quarters: never lesser coins. The counting machine at the Jewel supermarket at all times has a long line of characters. It's like a social club where everyone makes everyone else more alive, but less jumpy. Coinstar tithes 10 percent of what you pour into it and it's involving to pour the change in, to catch the spraying rejects and try again. The woman ahead of me glanced over and said, "Everything helps." She poured her change from tall tins that had once held incense or Pringles.

(MÁRQUEZ [1967] 2006)

Media Trouble

One of the parents tells the others, in shock, that the kids have been sexting. But when I check her texts, it's all, "Hi, meet me over there" then days or weeks later, "I CAN'T BE YOUR FRIEND ANYMORE!!!!!" then again, "Hi, what are you doing?" I ask her why she keeps breaking up with her friends. She says she doesn't remember and launches into an impenetrable side stream. I realize that whatever's happening is distributed across platforms—Minecraft, Animal Jam, Instagram, recess. Not the kind of thing that lends itself to helicopter forensics. The moms say, "Drama! I'd like to knock their heads together." But we're all in too.

They play fake dating games that get real and end in mountains of shame and blame. There's profound humiliation and wilding retaliation and we can't even figure out what happened. She was hurt when she tried to get support from her friends after her car accident and they texted back "cool." One accused her of "fake crying." We had a talk about preteen awkwardness but within hours her best friend was screaming at her for saying "whoopee" at the news that she'd been selected for a solo in a musical.

Hundreds do things

Hundreds do things with movement, pattern, and concept; hundreds stretch out a scene, hold up a world's jelling, and register change, which is not the antithesis of chains. They're an operation without a tone of voice you'd expect, like the sonnet whose couplet resists a capture, the dozens that play black excellence, baby! for the torque and surprising norm, the calendrical poem that says WRITING WAS HERE at a place-time that loose-hinges what a stranger could know to the density of something shared. We call them poems because they're about making. Because language is such a force from the world we jerry-rig figures and fiddle with pulse to make things accessible. A play on is what we have to work with, parts reaching out to other ones in lateral spray, toward time's fronts and backs, or stilled, broken and present: because we are historical. The freedom of loving is like this swerving ongoing transcranial fishing for our unshakable relational singularity, which includes our tropes. What are we going to do with our proximity, baby!? Worlds and scenes and poems come from it, and a sense of what counts and builds out, the metrics. We, too, make tracks for potential sync.

(S. ANDERSON 2016)

Survivors in Training

JUNE

I know you know the body has autonomous events, blips and bloops. It's all dynamic and a thing happens that induces another thing whether or not you sense it, want it, feel happy about it, love being chewed up and spit out by it, scratch an itch unconsciously, eat candy or take a handful of nuts because the good object hides the shameful motive that brings you to be absorbed in it. I hear Affect Theory announces that life persists throughout moments. But why is that a thing to say? June's worn makeup to the gym each Sunday since after her mother died suddenly. It is a summer afternoon and the world we live in involves friends walking tightly around the inside of the track to make room for the runners. Gestures and floating phrases add up or not, until in the badly lit steam room she opens up about caretaking and chemo, invented for war as a killing poison. Turns out they're all survivors but I'm grinning too, although I can't say for sure if it's at this scene or something else, like the sensation of my beautifully fitted sneakers, silver-gray and snug like a snake with a mouse in it.

TY

Ty is always in training. He is huge like a skyscraper's grand front door, ambitious to expand and twist like a looming python in full hood that can block out the sun. He is a body builder; he is slowly becoming blind. He says, "I'm black but I only eat white food." In the square Tupperware with the tight blue top there are egg whites and white rice. Today is his birthday and he asked me to tell you that he will never give up, never. We are gym rats together. I met him at the gym when he was seventeen; he was the kind of kid who asked Big Questions. Men trained him; women fed him. I helped him with homework and applications. Today he asked me to describe him to you. His mind is always working, like the Egyptians who chew khat and squat all day. In the beginning they all chewed six hours a day, now it's just the chosen few. Ty's got a theory of everything and has a lot to say. He works at least two jobs each day. This is his life, a magic carpet that thrums on a bumpy sky.

(MALABOU 2012)

Two young men with beards kissing on the floor.

A man with a beard walked in and kissed his boyfriend, who was lying on the floor in a brown coat. The reclining man wore a hoodie and bright earplugs a different color than his skin. All the people in the room were on the floor with earplugs, but not all were bearded or greeted by a bearded boyfriend whose passionate kiss arced in a beeline to the head he cradled for a shorter time than it takes to describe them, the brown-dressed bearded men, one of them white, kissed in the crook of an arm on the face.

Refractions

An enigma that is also an overfilling of form renders its "we" a voice of contagious reiteration. A mystery path entrains a problematic, pressing materials into service. Some people become its crazy or a refraction of its tempo or some chaos of possibilities.

Others are amazed by all this, if they even notice.

What counts as the social now has sound effects, like a metronome's tick. Talking about it is like talking about ghosts or auras or power.

Evaluative critique is a mental habit of demagnetizing things for the sake of clarity. Try remagnetizing and then think again.

Reading Notes, the Week of December 16, '16

1. A dog embodies what in being will choke itself on its leash. (BOTTOMS 2008)
2. Allegory is a puddle of remnants imitating a membrane. (W. BENJAMIN 1999)
3. Poetry is an idea of a diffuse action settling for a mood. (JACKSON 2005)
4. Breathing is what dodged a bullet if you're lucky. (TREMBLAY 2018)
5. Sickness is to an image of life what the imitation of style is to writing. (BELLAMY 2015)
6. Everyone needs a project or they might die, or become literal. (SEARCH PARTY)
7. The mustard color was so intense that it read as a racial membrane. (MERPORT 2017)
8. Some sentences suck the world in and become drunk with detail. (DANGO 2017)
9. I wanted to smear myself all over the world so that I would never miss you, but I keep missing YOU. (BROWNING 2012)
10. Ariana and the dog are loud and jumpy; I needed a space to love without dry ice. (STEWART 2007)
11. Here's another tableau of intimacy that won't respond to questions. (LEPSELTER 2014)
12. Draw what you can't say yet. (CAUSEY 2016)
13. The *riot*, the *dialectic*, *not* giving up, *showing* up. (CLOVER 2016)
14. I promise. (TRUMP 2016)
15. Joyous violence without the masks of reason is truly the end of trust. (THE HISTORICAL PRESENT)
16. A world in crisis where indifference is impossible turns out not to exist. (WILDERSON, WITH BALL, BURROUGHS, AND HATE 2014)
17. We wish for evidence the way we wish to use love—to simplify and let us be good-natured sometimes. (WHITEHEAD 1999)
18. Love is food that makes you emptier than food with no qualities, which makes you fuller. (KLEEMAN 2015)
19. Love involves wanting people to get what they want. (LEGIT 2013–2014)

20. Love and power, where your mind goes first thing in the morning. (HOOKS 2000)

21. Secrets and manners sustain families and slaveries. (SPILLERS 2003)

22. All psychosis is sociopathy but not all craziness is. (W. J. T. MITCHELL, FORTHCOMING)

23. Love is hate and so is hate. (AHMED 2003)

24. Locally sourced savory pretzel stuffed with Ham & Cheese. (KAFEIN)

25. I believed x because I needed to stay in the room. (HOANG 2016)

26. You can't trust in theory: take wordplay. (COMEDY)

27. The stain, you can't wash it away. (LETINSKY AND MORABITO 2015)

28. The way we solve problems involves capping what leaks. (SCAPPETONE 2016)

29. Shitshow, clusterfuck. (OVERHEARD AT A PROTEST)

30. Schadenfreude comes to me, harries me, hooks me, militates the mind. (PRINCE 1988; SIMON 2017)

31. Open my heart to better defenses. (QUOTE UNQUOTE)

32. Beach vacation versus hibernation! (TAXICAB)

33. Your ad on this bench! (AFTER THE TAXICAB)

34. Passing between another's body and yours, not lecturing. (WINNICOTT [1971] 1982)

35. Aloneness is a fundamental inalterable state of boundlessness that allows you to feel confident that the world persists alongside your noise and shredded confidence. (EIGEN 2004)

36. Psychopaths identify the world as its holes. (EIGEN 2004)

37. The desire to catch the drift. (OGDEN 1997)

38. I see the object in the distance but I lose confidence. (WRITERS)

39. Comedy reduces speech to nonsense and politics converts nonsense to speech. (FREUD [1905] 1960; RANCIÈRE 2011)

Just being me

I'm in Boulder and in the hotel hallway there's a framed photograph of Bob Dylan's face above an antique table and a vase of flowers. The lacy handwritten caption reads, "All I can do is be me, whoever that is." The "me" is a mass of reactions vaguely jarred into being at the glimpse of a method or a thought. Just trying to catch up with whatever's happening, it sloughs off retroactive dreams of itself, like old skin. It's a recombinant unfolding but with a life of its own. It likes to swim; it hates to wait; it wants raspberries.

Office Hours

The Hundreds is not just "where does the misery come from?" as we sense the felt tip of the world drawing figures, hooks, and asterisks. It's also about what happens when we stop saying "affect is in the world" as though the phrase resolves the writing of impact, spring, and relation. You have to and can't trust yourself with placing what's structural, technical, transferential, pulped, leaking, intense.

One day I was late, despite a New Year's resolution to be early always. I admit I was irritated that this student had insisted on an inconvenient time, so when I say that my lateness was unintentional I have no ground from which to speak. I dash into the café with the silver light where I like to hold an hour because it's public and no one can feel more trapped. It's a white room with a high glass ceiling whose purpose, I've been told, is to show that the sky is no limit. We sit at a white table on white chairs made of a metal infrastructural grid. The inadequate cushions are Ad Reinhardt black. The designers imagined a still life, not a lifeworld where we show up to build things out.

It is hard to focus on her because I'm palpitating and she's a blur to herself. Her language moves sideways into hesitation. Students all around us are hugging and fist-bumping. She looks tired and there's a cake makeup layer that points to what it isn't hiding. Her live idea is that celebrities want to be famous but not to be known. We rack our brains to convert this interest into a research question. On reflection it appears that she hates people who have pushy curiosity and also people who don't.

You can decide not to be known or to be disappointed mostly in the way you are known, I said.

While we were talking, my next hour walked in. The hair on this specific vector of warmth is shiny, made brittle by too much product. She walks in tights and a roving sweater. When she comes over to let us know it is time I see her teeth worn to china disks. The archive of bulimia smiles and the meth mouth's jagged edges crashes in and my already wrung heart really, not metaphorically, aches into the generosity of the impersonal silence that allows us to focus on what *can* be done.

Survival of the fittest means a different thing now, not all of it bad or good, and not all of it something that has an opposite.

In the book *Mildred Pierce* the eponymous one was a little dense. She thought a good business would allow her to bank some love. One daughter died of an acne infection that began in the triangle around the mouth. The person who told me this said it in bed one night with a tensed-up face. I am falling asleep as I type, as this is getting close to a thing about learning whose pressure on attention is exhausting.

One time a student asked me to "rip to shreds" their overworked yet dormant object. "Is that what I do?" I asked. "Deadline" derives from the line drawn around a prison that permits a police sniper to shoot if a prisoner crosses over without permission. Another time someone confessed they were poor, and that their mother was a hairdresser. Another time a student was condescending, so I gave them their echo to play with. Another time we were watching a movie and students rebelled because I watched the credits in the dark till the end.

(J. BENJAMIN 1998; CAIN [1941] 1989; MOTEN 2008A, 2008B; POE 1846; ROSE 1989; STILLINGER 1991; WINNICOTT [1971] 1982)

Under Pressure

Sociality is a thing under pressure. Before, beside, after all the rules and the roles, it's a rhythm marking the beat of a saturation no one's just in or out of. Charged by the manic labors of keeping up with what's at hand and bowled over by the torque of things, its too-muchness is also a deficiency but not something to sneer at.

Some look for a method. You keep your water glass in the same place on the bed stand for your hand to grope in the night, you shrink-wrap yourself when someone comes at you, you decide to sit this one out, you try to get out there and interact, or talking to people in an encounter is a way to make and hold up the noise of the world.

The so-called big picture is something else where now, somehow, the punishing realism of best practices gets to elbow in, posturing at a centering but all that's really centered is power's force, plain and simple. There are claims to knowledge, some knowledge is unbearable and a threat to living. There are safeties for thought—concepts held in common, the rediscovery of a well-known logic in a scene that might have done something else if it could have.

But our method is not that. It's a co-compose pushing off a cut or a story, finishing a thought in play, editing down to the momentary but perfect capture that's not just a characterization but the machinery of generation. The point for us is not to track things into their secret lairs but to see what could happen in singular thought-events. Ours is a thought experiment of thought experiments. Being overwhelmed makes a different kind of sense. In a starting point things jump into relation but remain unglued.

Once my mother's father dropped his four little girls at school a town over and never came back. After school they stood on the sidewalk together. Then they started walking. They asked a stranger for a nickel so they could get something to drink. They didn't know where they were going. By the time she was ten my mother was driving his truck all over town, not that she wanted to. I wonder what the stranger with the nickel thought.

There was an act/body. There was a thought. Something happening shifted on its weight. There was back talk, decomp. The Jell-O jelled.

("UNDER PRESSURE" 1982)

Ordinary Love

In the dream we took turns being inconvenient to each other, so the dream was good social theory. It wasn't pleasant—domesticity was a big mood swing. Downstairs, two black women and a white man our age made gigantic sculptures impossible to see from any angle: it was a cooperative and everyone took each other gently. Our ginger cat climbed up the door and squeezed into the space at the top. I became afraid to leave, to lose more things. The next day the internet was down: as usual we were forced to work with freshly approximate knowledge.

Now the feeling my body's holding seems like a good because it's holding me, but that's bad theory. It's not just holding that's good or being held: also play and wandering. Among the puns cut away were holing chamber. Among the edits were many words after "held." Since my cat died I've also stopped wanting to spend money. Paradoxically, I've been fixing up things I'd let go, and we all know delay always ends up costing. I've turned around and in that turning face nothing but the twist that can't be fixed by strong arms. It was nice to feel that much love.

(MCEWEN 1998; PUCK)

Stocking Up

The Salvation Army is our mother lode. Cross-country skis for five dollars a pair, little china plates for twenty-five cents. The old bookshelf won't fit in the car. We stand there looking at it. A woman in a truck smiles at us and then pauses near us as she's walking into the store. The manager comes out to put something in her car. "How's it going?" "Oh, ya know, a manager's life is open to close." Me: "We can't get this in the car." "Don't you know anyone with a truck?" "No, we're new." She stands by sympathetically for a minute but I can't tell if she's keeping us company or sticking to a company policy of no returns.

The woman from the truck comes back out. "Are you going local?" "Ya." "Put it in the back. I'll follow you." "Wait . . . What? . . . No. We're going all the way over to Gilford on 11A. It's far." "It's OK, I know the area." I drive gingerly, watching her in the rearview mirror, not sure what I'm worried about but there's weight. When we get there I can see she's very emotional too; I give her twenty dollars. Her eyes light up and she shakes a little. I give her a hug. Me: "Thank you so much. You made my day." "Oh, that's OK. Welcome to New Hampshire. I'm a pay-it-forward kind of person and like I told Mike when I walked into the store, the proverb was kind of long to memorize today, could I read it twice out loud and get the 10 percent off, and he said sure. So it all works out." I try to rise to the occasion of her gleam. She's small, thin, French-Canadian-looking. Later, our condo manager confirms that this is what people here do.

Bad Weather

Two women with skin like construction workers and middle-aged pony-tails were eating pretzels and mustard in the airport bar, 5:30AM. One carried a quilted white porthole purse and the other carried a military backpack with everything you could ever want in case you're stranded, plus beer. It was like I had landed on a desert island "spacious without the need for verification of space." Porthole says, we are best friends, we should be married, our husbands—what are you going to do with men who won't move? My grin drops a quarter in the complaint machine and talk sets flight.

(CHA [1982] 2009)

In it

We write to be in the reverb of word and world.

From the start we committed to the composition and decomp in every-thing, we took the long way around. We tried on other keys, feeling out the timing for a joke, working the angle on what describes and hovers. Dropping the diagnostic tone even for a minute brought surprise, attitude voiceovers; perspective became precise. We worked subsentence, looking for phrasing and a sense. Impressions reshaped a thought practice. Refrains looped back and unraveled slowly.

We made a method of sounding things out, rolling over words as if we could curl our tongues on them, whispering "choo choo" as we laid down a track. We tried different points of emphasis, cutting and stretching a sentence, sacrificing adjectives and metaphors in favor of the right sonic sequence. We developed relationships to our own and each other's word sounds. Katie wanted to get the world some attention. She became a letter writer writing of a world to a world. Lauren wanted all the knowledge of a place to converge. She bargained for precision with rhythm and beauty.

We write to invite and to goad, to bring the weight of scenes home; not to model.

A Number on Introductions

I am so happy to introduce to you this esteemed stranger. Once they would strategize the fate of the world: now they worry about the force of words.

Once I read a thing by this person that shifted some other things and changed stuff that I saw later, and not just in books. My sense of implications was so jacked up it was "as though I were constantly vomiting but had no mouth."

This person's work is often funny, as in "this milk tastes funny." A pun pushes your tongue into the bad taste of your drive toward it. It pulls you back into artless play. It sours when your persistent interest leaks. But wait—that's how Frank and Sedgwick describe shame! CSI: When Generalizations Meet. Our concepts penetrate each other till they're "in the air."

My colleague never calls before arriving to town. It's ungracious for me to whine in public about this, but a sense of abandonment is just another name for frustrated attachment, where Bion locates the primal scene of thinking. They promise to theorize the revolution that will happen if we pay attention. They promise a talk that will fuel us for the next wars of attrition.

(BION 1959; FRANK AND SEDGWICK 1995; SOLOMON 1998)

A month in arrests and other things

In one month in some coal mining camps in West Virginia I wrote down these things I heard:

1. Someone broke into Della Mae's and stole fifty dollars, pickled eggs, and pinto beans.
2. Someone burned Charlie's house; his daughter's doll collection melted.
3. Pete Shrewsbury and a boy from Killarney were arrested.
4. Someone pulled the wire on the water pump in Rhodell.
5. Ronnie Alexander died of pills and liquor, his father left them when he was two, he went to school through third grade, he drank a lot before he married at nineteen, he had eight kids, he saw things in the woods.
6. Sam Tanks's son beat him up bad.
7. Elanda Hamlet was almost raped by William Street.
8. Zackie Shrewsbury spent a day in court. He worked in the mines, in lumbering, on the railroad. One son drank himself to death in Chicago, a daughter died of diphtheria, another daughter is nervous; she tingles.
9. Etta Spangler's husband was indicted for grand larceny for stealing cars. She had thirteen kids, her uterus hangs out of her body; when I called her to ask about getting some firewood she opened with a ten-minute monologue on planting by the signs.
10. He always takes a red-hot shower. Most of the accidents in the mines are caused by carelessness. He smashed a finger and broke a toe from the spewing rock; they call it inactive. There was no job or safety training. They'd go to their cars to drink, they'd smoke in the mines. Don't drink in the mines; the air pressure makes you sick. Once there was a fire, a loud whooshing sound like a train coming. He stayed in until he realized the foreman didn't know what he was doing and then he got out.
11. She had three marriages; at one point she stopped eating meat because she thought she had to for her hypertension. She has numbness and tingling.

12. Many lost houses, cars, furniture, during the last strike. This one will be easier because people will have tax returns.
13. There was a house fire; a screaming baby was trapped inside.
14. A description of what a flood did to a house.

I always wondered what this litany did, but if I tried to get at it they'd say, "I don't have no ideal, Katie," and then they'd have to start over.

Not Over Yet

You take the factory with you when you leave the factory town, the tinny smell of defrosted chicken shivering in its final moment. Telephones, too, remind you that you used to be willing to tether to something, even to lift the receiver to hear the ex say that you're still a piece of shit. But it's not over yet. Everywhere you went there was love and other kinds of dispossession. Everywhere you went you had urges without plans and sometimes you made plans. You can look around where you're sitting now and know that what's there isn't all of it.

(BION 1959; CONRAD 2014; HIGHSMITH [1962] 2011)

II. Indexes

Index · *Fred Moten*

There's too much pointed repeating to point at, being caught up in it.
   The overall is all over
the place, numberless in thick and thin. No place to go is all over the
   place. Shifters, riffless
because the splits are staggered, get their drink on. Echoes can't get
   located, obvious things
gone aviary, map flown all over the place. We're missing the overall.
   You're missing the overall,

this way free that way green, stuck way out like this, when don you
   know de day's erbroad?
Outnumbered, parenthetical finger pointing around the corner, won't
   straighten all up in can't
straighten how you straighten up in the morning, all your voices un-
   raveling while your voices
lounge in the overall, what pleasure had these tracks laid down? Nothing but all that shifting,

how the road turns over the edge of anything you be trying to do. Let's
   call this song exactly
what it is. In lieu of its name let's call it you, or y'all. All y'all up in there
   started flying out of
place, started missing, started can't get started, won't fly right, can't get
   it straight, can't turn
it loose but there it go and now it's gone and there y'all go again, can
   call it but can't point to it.

Y'all keep saying that's what I'm talking 'bout don't even sound right
   and now you want an
index? And that's just what y'all be always talking 'bout with all the
   voices in your voices and
their outstretched hands. The overall is alert to this dancing more than
   singing, y'all said, and

there's a hand jive with some presence in it all throughout but no place
    special, off to the side,

glancing at all the colors in thirty-third. Level, degree, flickering resource
    back and forth all over
the place, amarillo all over the place as sunlight, called exactly what it
    is but pointed out only so
we can say what it feels when we describe it, get it all down to the
    point of it being all y'all all
over the damn place. It feels terribly beautiful. It feels terribly beauti-
    ful. Everywhere you went.

Not-Index · *Andrew Causey and C. Thresher*

PART OF THIS STORY YOU HAVE TO TELL YOURSELF

THE DREAD OF BEING INSIDE AN UNNAMEABLE ENORMITY

What did they *actually* say?, 80, 87, 116

Detours: things that turn out to have, 44, 85

Workhorses: backing away from, 92

Circuits: comfort found in, 28

Breathing, no room for, 110

Tableau, life is not a, 8

Sourings, *passim*

THINGS PILE UP: SWELLING, BLISTERING

Trash bags: being dragged; being hidden, 91

Premonitions: swells of, *passim*

Sinking: feeling of, worrying about, dreams, *passim*
Smells: tinny, of love, 81, 135
Transformations: holding back, *passim*
Staying out of it: can't, 100

Why bother to intervene?, 133
Rescue: is there?, 108
Rejects being spewed, 115

Holes: world defined by its, 122
Crazy things sit next together, *passim*

GOT A GIFT, DID A FAVOR: THINGS ARE STARTING TO JELL

Not sure, which is which?, *passim*

Something: trying to get away with, 83
False cheer: trying out, 43
When to open our wings?, 109

Burrowing: safety of; exploration of, 95
Tight spot: climbing into, staying in, 128

Play: existing, need to play with, *passim*

Bags: packed, just in case, 130

Big enough to be described, 30, 47, 97

Typing: falling asleep while, 125

Earplugs: kissing while wearing, 119

The Index · *Susan Lepselter*

Nathaniel Bagshaw Ward, an English botanist, accidentally invented the terrarium in 1842. In his glass case meant for insects, a spore of fern took hold and grew. He called it the Wardian case. Allow him please to demonstrate the wonder. Heat and light enter the glass, water evaporates inside, vapor gathers on the walls, falling back to the ferns below. Jesus Christ. Sometimes it's all too much. Walking on the beach we watch the tide go in and out and in. Patterns form. We have come to this house for decades. Now some of us are old. Cans of soup line the shelf. *We ask our readers to perform the jamb when language overruns the mental breathing that reading entails.* No one said the Wardian case has to fit on a desk, or in a town. In my city the floods begin, the streets give way to rivers. A wooly mammoth once pissed as it ran. Nothing completely disappears. My city will dry up, and the rain will come to yours. My dog is drinking a puddle. *We make a pass at a swell in realism, and look for the hook. We back up at the hint of something.* My sister and I had not spoken in months; the hurt swelled. Yesterday we finally talked for hours and she sobbed into the phone. Nothing was resolved. I felt ripples from a rape in the seventeenth century, behind a barn somewhere in Romania, where generations later my bitter grandmother disparaged her children without knowing why. Nothing disappears. Resentment wafted like a gas in the house. No one noticed. You breathe the air you're given. Stalking around cracked pavement ferns, this crow, with its strong beak and calculating eyes, resembles both a pterodactyl and my father. A girl lashes the wind with kelp. I stumble on aftershocks from a shock I can't point out.

Words sediment next to something laid low. The conversation builds; this epistolary novel is a poem. But already a poem is a conversation. A single word is dense with charges. Writing back and forth for years, two voices recalibrate and sync. Overlap and pull apart. Listen to this. Look. Index it. But don't point the finger, little judges. You remind me to point sideways, to the shapeless thing I want to name, the thing that hangs around. It shifts its shape. A shifter's only meaning is the object it happens to point to. The little girls pose with one hand bent from the wrist as if once in some other place or time this was the way a princess stood. *Melodramas of mixed ontological status hit swells of feeling and the force of things colliding.* You opened the window to get rid of the atmosphere; but the air just swelled. Come here and watch the vapors gather into clouds of the fiercest orange. A drop of mammoth pee still rides in that fleece. In their glass case Mr. Ward's ferns survived the performance of shipping to Australia—fringed, coiled seahorse tails, the green recycling, breathing. Oh come on, maybe a few of them died. It is just so fucking lonely here sometimes. *Go back, I suggest. You can never return, he says. I have to relearn life all over like a baby; it's so damn lonely.* Maybe the boys are throwing poppers. We walk on the dunes and forget the news of missiles. We just feel this recursive earth might break any day like a glass container, back to the particles of its birth.

Untitled · *Stephen Muecke*

The aesthetic, in its original meaning, is about sensitivities discovering their form. . . . And a sensitive child takes offense easily and then sulks for hours. So much seems to slip by, yet we want to cultivate the arts of attention so that important things don't get lost forever. Who decides? The makers of history are closer than you think. Some of them will agree to talk to you. They might have an agenda, or a program, as in, stick with it—or not. But pattern? Maybe, because of rhythm. Prepositions are matters of concern, or rather pivots: the intimacy of the *with*, rather than the military strategy of the *about*.

Having, rather than being. As in attachments, weak links. We can dance to one side of the identity politics of asking what it is, and instead ask, *What's it got going for it? What makes it persist?* Listen to Karen Dalton sing "Something on Your Mind": "I've seen the writing on the wall / Who can't maintain will always fail." The right kind of accessory matters, anyone can tell you that.

Stephen (texting Pru in airport departure lounge): "I'm feeling sad." Pru: "I felt sad too but it will be alright." And she adds, "I always panic in the lead up to a change and I managed the tsunami in my dream perfectly."

Who would ever think of indexing as a chore? When you have all that random power, and the publisher won't quibble. You can index words like "loitering." Or a friend's name that makes only a brief appearance in the acknowledgments, because of a fondness. Indexers "R" Us: all we literally do is point, that is why all this mob is getting crick necks. Style is another matter—no new thought without new style (Nietzsche). Here you go, Fred. Style is a test. Any objections? (Sort them all out, and you have a totally sick objectivity—Latour.) Yes, it is fictocriticism: The *ficto*-side of fictocriticism follows the twists and turns of animated language as it finds new pathways. The *-criticism* part comes in the risky leap of taking the story to a different "world," where it might be tested by an unexpected public.

The glitches are welcome interruptions that force a reset (like a robo-toy that hits the furniture, reverses, and turns left) so that the persistence can go again. And of course you wonder what the mechanism is, the system, the black-box magic. It *is* all there, after the performance you go backstage and the masks are off. Someone cries and you wonder about erotic undercurrents. Tomorrow, or later tonight, the masks will go on again, and again, slightly different each time.

Who needs a long narrative arc anyway, when fragments have their own subjective affordances? Long narratives are Wall Street investments in character. Literary monuments. But here there are hundreds of glimpses, flashes like in the fire opals from Lightning Ridge. A glimpse, a figure half seen in the mist, is an emergent concept or feeling that has its value in its evanescence.

For Your Indexing Pleasure

Some Things We Thought With

100-Word Collective (editor and co-author). 2013. *VIA: Voices in Italian Americana* 24 (1–2): 95–108.

1950s women's bathing suits.

A box of photographs once taken.

Abrams, Muhal Richard. 1968. "Bird Song." On *Levels and Degrees of Light.* Delmark, DD413, 1991, compact disc.

Adorno, Theodor. (1974) 1991. "On Lyric Poetry and Society." In *Notes to Literature, Volume 1,* edited by Rolf Tiedemann, translated by Shierry Weber Nicholsen, 37–54. New York: Columbia University Press.

Adorno, Theodor. (1951) 2005. *Minima Moralia: Reflections on a Damaged Life.* Translated by E. F. N. Jephcott. London: Verso.

A few pansies stuck in a window box.

A fuck-you shrug.

Agamben, Giorgio. (1996) 2000. *Means without End: Notes on Politics.* Translated by Vincenzo Binetti and Cesare Casarino. Minneapolis: University of Minnesota Press.

Agamben, Giorgio. 2009. "What Is a Paradigm?" In *The Signature of All Things: On Method,* translated by Luca D'Isanto with Kevin Attell, 9–32. New York: Zone Books.

Ahmed, Sara. 2003. "In the Name of Love." *borderlands e-journal* 2 (3). http://www.borderlands.net.au/vol2no3_2003/ahmed_love.htm.

Ainsworth, M. D. S., M. C. Blehar, E. Waters, and S. Wall. 1978. *Patterns of Attachment: A Psychological Study of the Strange Situation.* Hillsdale, NJ: Erlbaum.

Amplifying: a density, a sensitivity, a promise, a subtraction, a ricochet, breakthrough dreaming, a sideways glance, a side effect.

Anderson, Ben. 2009. "Affective Atmospheres." *Emotion, Space and Society* 2 (2): 77–81.

Anderson, Ben. 2016. *Encountering Affect: Capacities, Apparatuses, Conditions.* London: Routledge.

Anderson, Stephanie. 2016. "Dating the Poem, 1930–80: Toward a Calendrical Poetics." PhD diss., University of Chicago.

An egg-cooking machine.

Animatronic sparkle.

Anti-insanity phone calls.

A phrase in circulation.

Arendt, Hannah. 1958. "Irreversibility and the Power to Forgive." In *The Human Condition*, 236–42. Chicago: University of Chicago Press.

A shoulder twitching.

Attitude games.

Augé, Marc. (1992) 2009. *Non-Places: An Introduction to Supermodernity*. Translated by John Howe. London: Verso.

Baldwin, James. (1963) 1992. "My Dungeon Shook: Letter to My Nephew on the One Hundredth Anniversary of the Emancipation." In *The Fire Next Time*, 1–10. New York: Vintage.

Barad, Karen. 2003. "Posthumanist Performativity: Toward an Understanding of How Matter Comes to Matter." *Signs* 28 (3): 801–31.

Barry, Lynda. 2008. *What It Is*. Montreal: Drawn and Quarterly.

Barthes, Roland. (1973) 1975. *The Pleasure of the Text*. Translated by Richard Miller. New York: Hill and Wang.

Barthes, Roland. (1977) 1978. *A Lover's Discourse: Fragments*. Translated by Richard Howard. New York: Hill and Wang.

Barthes, Roland. (1980) 1981. *Camera Lucida: Reflections on Photography*. Translated by Richard Howard. New York: Hill and Wang.

Barthes, Roland. (2002) 2005. *The Neutral: Lecture Course at the Collège de France (1977–1978)*. New York: Columbia University Press.

Bathing suits. *See* women: the 1950s.

Baudelaire, Charles. 1857. "Au Lecteur." In *Fleurs du mal*. http://fleursdumal .org/poem/099.

Bellamy, Dodie. 2015. *When the Sick Rule the World*. Los Angeles: Semiotext(e).

Benjamin, Jessica. 1998. "What Angel Would Hear Me? The Erotics of Transference." In *Like Subjects, Love Objects: Essays on Recognition and Sexual Difference*, 143–74. New Haven, CT: Yale University Press.

Benjamin, Walter. 1999. *The Arcades Project*. Translated by Howard Eiland and Kevin McLaughlin. Cambridge, MA: Harvard University Press.

Berardi, Franco "Bifo." 2012. *The Uprising: On Poetry and Finance*. Los Angeles: Semiotext(e).

Bergson, Henri. (1900) 1914. *Laughter: An Essay on the Meaning of the Comic*. Translated by Cloudesley Brereton and Fred Rothwell. New York: Macmillan.

Bigger Than Life.

Bion, W. R. 1959. "Attacks on Linking." *International Journal of Psychoanalysis* 40:308–15.

Bishop, Elizabeth. (1955) 1983. "At the Fishhouses." In *The Complete Poems, 1927–1979,* 64–66. New York: Farrar, Straus and Giroux.

Blue glass vases.

Bolaño, Roberto. 2012. "Labyrinth." *New Yorker,* January 23. Accessed September 27, 2017. https://www.newyorker.com/magazine/2012/01/23/labyrinth-roberto-bolano.

Bollas, Christopher. 1992. *Being a Character: Psychoanalysis and Self-Experience.* New York: Hill and Wang.

Bottoms, Greg. 2008. *Fight Scenes.* Berkeley, CA: Counterpoint Press.

Bowler, Kate. 2013. *Blessed: A History of the American Prosperity Gospel.* New York: Oxford University Press.

Breakfasts.

Brooks, Gwendolyn. (1945) 1987. "Gay Chaps at the Bar." In *Blacks,* 64–75. Chicago: Third World Press.

Browning, Barbara. 2012. *I'm Trying to Reach You.* Columbus, OH: Two Dollar Radio Press.

Cadava, Eduardo, and Paola Cortés-Rocca. 2006. "Notes on Love and Photography." *October* 116:3–34.

Cahill, Zachary. 2014a. *WECANTMAKEYOUBETTER,* watercolor on paper, 9 × 12 in. Courtesy of the artist.

Cahill, Zachary. 2014b. *YOUNEEDEXHAUSTION,* limited edition poster produced for the Eighth Berlin Biennale for Contemporary Art: 9 PLUS 1, 27.75 × 39.5 in. Courtesy of the artist.

Cain, James M. (1941) 1989. *Mildred Pierce.* New York: Vintage.

Cantet, Laurent (director). 2001. *Time Out/L'emploi du temps.* Artificial Eye, 2002, DVD.

Captures: try to catch the drift.

Cats and dogs.

Causey, Andrew. 2016. *Drawn to See: Drawing as Ethnographic Method.* Toronto: University of Toronto Press.

Cha, Theresa Hak Kyung. (1982) 2009. *Dictee.* Berkeley: University of California Press.

Chickens.

Clough, Patricia. 2000a. *Autoaffection: Unconscious Thought in the Age of Technology*. Minneapolis: University of Minnesota Press.

Clough, Patricia. 2000b. "Comments on Setting Criteria for Experimental Writing." *Qualitative Inquiry* 6 (2): 278–91.

Clough, Patricia, and Jean Halley, eds. 2007. *The Affective Turn: Theorizing the Social*. Durham, NC: Duke University Press.

Clover, Joshua. 2016. *Riot. Strike. Riot: The New Era of Uprisings*. London: Verso.

Cohen, Lawrence. 2011. "Love and the Little Line." *Cultural Anthropology* 26 (4): 692–96.

Conrad, C. A. 2014. *Ecodeviance: (soma)tics for the Future Wilderness*. Seattle: Wave Books.

Contact aesthetic.

Contagion.

Cover stories.

Crawford, Romi. 2017. "Radical Relations! Memory, Objects, and the Generation of the Political." Lecture given at the Center for the Study of Gender and Sexuality, University of Chicago, February 6.

Culler, Jonathan, ed. 1988. *On Puns: The Foundation of Letters*. New York: Blackwell.

Dango, Michael. 2017. "Contemporary Styles: A Taxonomy of Novel Actions." PhD diss., University of Chicago.

Daniel, Drew. 2017. "Self-Killing and the Matter of Affect in Bacon and Spinoza." In *Affect Theory and Early Modern Texts: Politics, Ecologies, and Form*, edited by Amanda Bailey and Mario DiGangi, 89–108. London: Palgrave.

Davis, Lydia. 2010. *The Collected Stories of Lydia Davis*. New York: Picador Press.

Deleuze, Gilles. 1986. *Kafka: Toward a Minor Literature*. Minneapolis: University of Minnesota Press.

Deleuze, Gilles. (1988) 1993. "What Is an Event?" In *The Fold: Leibniz and the Baroque*, translated by Tom Conley, 76–82. Minneapolis: University of Minnesota Press.

Deleuze, Gilles. (1990) 1995. "Postscript on Control Societies." In *Negotiations*, translated by Martin Joughin, 177–82. New York: Columbia University Press.

Deleuze, Gilles, and Félix Guattari. (1972) 1983. *Anti-Oedipus: Capitalism and*

Schizophrenia. Translated by Robert Hurley, Mark Seem, and Helen R. Lane. Preface by Michel Foucault. Minneapolis: University of Minnesota Press.

Deleuze, Gilles, and Félix Guattari. 1987. *A Thousand Plateaus*. Translated by Brian Massumi. Minneapolis: University of Minnesota Press.

Deleuze, Gilles, and Félix Guattari. (1991) 1994. "Percept, Affect, and Concept." In *What Is Philosophy?*, translated by Hugh Tomlinson and Graham Burchell, 163–99. New York: Columbia University Press.

Detours, threads, gestures, reverb, leftovers.

de Zengotita, Thomas. 2006. *Mediated: How the Media Shapes Your World and How You Live In It*. London: Bloomsbury.

Diaconu, Mădălina. 2006. "Patina—Atmosphere—Aroma: Towards an Aesthetics of Fine Differences." *Analecta Husserliana* 92:131–48.

Dillard, Annie. 1975. *Pilgrim at Tinker Creek*. New York: Bantam Books.

Dog walking.

Doty, Mark. 2010. *The Art of Description: World into Word*. Minneapolis, MN: Graywolf Press.

Eigen, Michael. 2004. *The Electrified Tightrope*. Edited by Adam Phillips. London: Karnac Books.

Ericson, Corwin. 2011. *Swell*. Seattle: Dark Coast Press.

Ericson, Corwin. 2013. *Checked Out OK*. Hadley, MA: Factory Hollow Press.

"Everything is gonna be alright." Overheard in pop songs. 1961. Rick Pappas and Prentis Slade (Richard Nichols) (first copyright holders), March 20. *Catalog of Copyright Entries*, Library of Congress (EU0000662930).

Evidence. *See* inventory; *see* love; *see* contact; *see* syntax.

Experiment but then a mouth or a hand commits. You try to keep yourself open. Things happen. A mind shadowing itself.

Expressivity thresholds.

Facebook.

Fire escape.

Fish, Stanley. 2012. *How to Write a Sentence: And How to Read One*. New York: Harper.

Fonagy, Peter, and Mary Target. 2007. "Playing with Reality: IV. A Theory of External Reality Rooted in Intersubjectivity." *International Journal of Psychoanalysis* 88:917–37.

Form of life.

Forms and genres and double takes, oh my.

Forrester, John. 2007. "On Kuhn's Case: Psychoanalysis and the Paradigm." *Critical Inquiry* 33 (4): 782–819.

Foucault, Michel. 1997. "Friendship as a Way of Life." In *Ethics: Subjectivity and Truth*, vol. 1 of *Essential Works of Foucault 1954–1984*, edited by Paul Rabinow, translated by Robert Hurley, 135–40. New York: New Press.

Four boxes of cranberry bread mix.

François, Anne-Lise. 2008. *Open Secrets: The Literature of Uncounted Experience*. Palo Alto, CA: Stanford University Press.

Frank, Adam, and Eve Kosofsky Sedgwick. 1995. "Shame in the Cybernetic Fold." *Critical Inquiry* 21 (2): 496–522.

Freckles.

Freud, Sigmund. (1905) 1960. *Jokes and Their Relation to the Unconscious*. In *The Standard Edition of the Complete Psychological Works*, volume 8, edited and translated by James Strachey, 9–236. London: Hogarth Press.

Freud, Sigmund. (1925) 1961. "A Note Upon the 'Mystic Writing-Pad.'" In *The Standard Edition of the Complete Psychological Works*, volume 19, edited and translated by James Strachey, 227–32. London: Hogarth Press.

Fuck. *See* shit. *See also* painkillers; swells.

Gamble, Kenny, Leon Huff, and Carey Gilbert. 1972. "Me and Mrs. Jones." Originally performed by Billy Paul. Philadelphia, PA: Philadelphia International Records ZS7 3521, 45 RPM.

Generative misperception.

Geronimi, Clyde, Wilfred Jackson, and Hamilton Luske (directors). 1951. *Alice in Wonderland*. Walt Disney Video, 2000, DVD.

Getting it, getting into it.

Gibbs, Anna. 2003. "Writing and the Flesh of Others." *Australian Feminist Studies* 18 (42): 309–19.

Gibbs, Anna. 2005. "Fictocriticism, Affect, Mimesis: Engendering Differences." *TEXT: Journal of the Australian Association of Writing Programs* 9, no. 1. http://www.textjournal.com.au/april05/gibbs.htm.

Gibbs, Anna. 2006. "Writing and Danger: The Intercorporeality of Affect." In *Creative Writing: Theory Beyond Practice*, edited by Nigel Krauth and Tess Brady, 157–68. Teneriffe, Australia: Post Pressed.

Gibbs, Anna. 2011. "Affect Theory and Audience." In *The Handbook of Media Audiences*, edited by Virginia Nightingale, 251–66, Oxford: Wiley-Blackwell.

Gillespie, Haven, and J. Fred Coots. 1938. "You Go to My Head." Newport Beach, CA: Haven Gillespie Music and Warner Brothers.

Gladman, Renée. 2016. *Calamities*. Seattle: Wave Books.

Glass, silver-rimmed ashtrays with snowflakes/abstract geometric designs on their bottoms.

Goffman, Erving. 1981. *Forms of Talk*. Philadelphia: University of Pennsylvania Press.

Gopnik, Adam. 2015. "The Outside Game." *New Yorker*, January 12.

Greenwell, Garth. 2016. *What Belongs to You*. New York: Farrar, Straus and Giroux.

Grinning.

Guattari, Félix. (1989) 2014. *The Three Ecologies*. Translated by Ian Pindar and Paul Sutton. London: Bloomsbury.

Habits you make or they land on you, not belonging to anyone.

Hamilton, Ann (artist). 2012–. *ONEEVERYONE*. Austin, TX.

Harman, Graham. 2008. "DeLanda's Ontology: Assemblage and Realism." *Continental Philosophical Review* 41 (3): 367–83.

Harman, Graham. 2011. "Realism without Materialism." *SubStance* 40 (2): 52–72.

Harman, Graham. 2012. *Weird Realism: Lovecraft and Philosophy*. Winchester, UK: Zero Books.

Harney, Stefano, and Fred Moten. 2013. *The Undercommons: Fugitive Planning and Black Study*. Wivenhoe, UK: Minor Compositions.

Hejinian, Lyn. (1980) 2002. *My Life*. Los Angeles: Green Integer Press.

Heuristics physics: stretching, loosening, tightening, sifting, moving with, attending, eddying, rigging, pointing toward, implying, thought experimenting, blueprinting. If the word "ekphrasing" exists, *see* ekphrasing.

Highsmith, Patricia. (1962) 2011. *The Cry of the Owl*. New York: Grove Press.

Hints (as in a hint of sour or vanilla; glances).

Hoang, Lily. 2016. *A Bestiary*. Cleveland, OH: Cleveland State University Poetry Center.

Hobbes, Thomas. (1651) 1991. *Leviathan*. Edited by Richard Tuck. Cambridge: Cambridge University Press.

Homer. 2016. *The Odyssey*. Translated by Anthony Verity. Oxford: Oxford University Press.

hooks, bell. 2000. *All About Love: New Visions*. New York: Harper.

Hopper, Edward (painter).

Howard Johnson's.

Hunter, Holly: said in *Top of the Lake* season one, episode seven, "All you hear are your own crazy thoughts like a river of shit, on and on. See your thoughts for what they are. Stop your helping. Stop your planning. Give up!"

Immersions—unintended, serial, unnoticed.

Impeckable Aviaries. Johnson City, Texas.

Ingold, Tim. 2015. *The Life of Lines*. London: Routledge.

Instagram.

"Jack and the Beanstalk."

Jackalope Coffee & Tea House. 755 W. 32nd St., Chicago, IL 60616. Storefront.

Jackson, Virginia. 2005. *Dickinson's Misery: A Theory of Lyric Reading*. Princeton, NJ: Princeton University Press.

Jacobus, Mary. 1995. *First Things: The Maternal Imaginary in Literature, Art, and Psychoanalysis*. London: Routledge.

Jain, S. Lochlann. 2013. *Malignant: How Cancer Becomes Us*. Berkeley: University of California Press.

Johnson, Liza (director). 2009. *In the Air*. Super 16 mm to HDCAM, 22 min.

Kafein. 1621 Chicago Ave. Evanston, IL, 60201.

Katchadourian, Nina (artist). 1998. Mended Spiderweb series.

Kerouac, Jack. (1957) 2012. *On the Road*. New York: Penguin Books.

Killed kids.

Kleeman, Alexandra. 2015. *You Too Can Have a Body Like Mine*. New York: Harper.

Klein, Melanie, and Joan Riviere. 1964. *Love, Hate and Reparation*. New York: Norton.

Knap, texture, sediment, shrinkage.

Knowing states: sharp, surprised, surprising, heavy, dissipated, disappointed, fascinated, not forever, fickle, motivated, clueless. *See also* rushed, as in adrenaline.

Koestenbaum, Wayne. 2011. *Humiliation*. New York: Picador.

Kozloff, Sarah. 1989. *Invisible Storytellers: Voice-Over Narration in American Fiction Film*. Berkeley: University of California Press.

Kusserow, Adrie. 2017. "Anthropoetry." In *Crumpled Paper Boat: Experiments in Ethnographic Writing*, edited by Anand Pandian and Stuart McLean, 71–90. Durham, NC: Duke University Press.

Kwon, Oh-sung (director). 2004. *Doggy-Poo*. 30 min. South Korea: Itasca Studio Inc.

Lacan, Jacques. 1991. *The Seminar of Jacques Lacan, Book 1: Freud's Papers on Technique 1953–1954*. Edited by Jacques-Alain Miller. Translated by John Forrester. New York: Norton.

Lahr, John. 2014. "Caught in the Act." *New Yorker*, September 15.

Laplanche, Jean. 1999. *Essays on Otherness*. Translated and edited by John Fletcher. London: Routledge.

Latour, Bruno. 1997. "A Few Steps Toward an Anthropology of the Iconoclastic Gesture." *Science in Context* 10 (1): 63–84.

Latour, Bruno. 2010. "An Attempt at a Compositionist Manifesto." *New Literary History* 41 (3): 471–90.

Laymon, Kiese. 2013. *How to Slowly Kill Yourself and Others in America*. Evanston, IL: Agate Bolden.

Lee, Stewart. 2014. "Reality is too full. Reality is too full, isn't it. Reality. There's too much stuff everywhere, in reality, isn't it." From *Stewart Lee's Comedy Vehicle*. Series 3, episode 2. Aired March 8, BBC 2.

Legit (TV series). 2013–2014. Created by Peter O'Fallon and Jim Jeffries. Starring Jim Jeffries, Dan Bakkedahl, D. J. Qualls. FX.

Lennon, John, and Paul McCartney. 1967. "A Day in the Life." Nashville, TN: Sony/ATV.

Lepselter, Susan. 2011. "The Disorder of Things: Hoarding Narratives in Popular Media." *Anthropological Quarterly* 84 (4): 919–48.

Lepselter, Susan. 2014. "Intimating Disaster: Apocalyptic Housekeeping from the Cold War Homemaker to the Neoliberal Hoarder." In *Reality Gendervision*, edited by Brenda Weber, 259–81. Durham, NC: Duke University Press.

Letinsky, Laura, and John Paul Morabito. 2015. *Stain: Eight Napkins with Variations*. http://lauraletinsky.com/stain/.

Light Brown M&M. Extinct (1995).

Linebaugh, Peter. 2008. *The Magna Carta Manifesto: Liberties and Commons for All*. Berkeley: University of California Press.

Lingis, Alphonso. 2015. "Irrevocable Loss." In *Non-Representational Methodologies: Re-Envisioning Research*, edited by Phillip Vannini, 165–76. New York: Routledge.

Little, Ken. 2012. "Belize Blues." *Semiotic Inquiry* 32 (1–2–3): 25–46.

Loeffler, Zachary John. 2018. "Speaking of Magic: Enchantment and Disenchantment in Music's Modernist Ordinary." Ph.D. dissertation. University of Chicago.

Lonely. *See* undertow; place.

Lyotard, Jean-François. 2004. "Anamnesis: Of the Visible." *Theory, Culture, and Society* 21 (1): 107–19.

Magic 8 Ball.

MagicBands.

Malabou, Catherine. 2011. *Changing Difference*. Cambridge: Polity Press.

Malabou, Catherine. 2012. *The New Wounded: From Neurosis to Brain Damage*. Translated by Steven Miller. New York: Fordham University Press.

Manning, Erin. 2009. *Relationscapes: Movement, Art, Philosophy*. Cambridge, MA: MIT Press.

Manning, Erin, and Brian Massumi. 2014. *Thought in the Act: Passages in the Ecology of Experience*. Minneapolis: University of Minnesota Press.

Marker, Chris. 2006. *The Case of the Grinning Cat*. 58 min. Brooklyn, NY: Icarus Films.

Márquez, Gabriel García. (1967) 2006. *One Hundred Years of Solitude*. Translated by Gregory Rabassa. New York: Harper.

Marx, Karl, and Friedrich Engels. (1848, 1888) 2008. *The Communist Manifesto*. Translated by Samuel Moore, with Friedrich Engels and Andy Blunden. Introduction by David Harvey. London: Pluto Books.

Massumi, Brian. 2010. "The Future Birth of the Affective Fact: The Political Ontology of Threat." In *The Affect Theory Reader*, edited by Melissa Gregg and Gregory J. Seigworth, 52–70. Durham, NC: Duke University Press.

Mavor, Carol. 2012. *Reading Boyishly: Roland Barthes, J. M. Barrie, Jacques Henri Lartigue, Marcel Proust, and D. W. Winnicott*. Durham, NC: Duke University Press.

Mayer, Bernadette. N.d. "Bernadette Mayer's List of Journal Ideas" and "Bernadette Mayer's Writing Experiments." http://www.writing.upenn.edu/library/Mayer-Bernadette_Experiments.html.

McCormack, Derek. 2013. *Refrains for Moving Bodies*. Durham, NC: Duke University Press.

McEwen, Ian. 1998. *Enduring Love*. New York: Anchor Books.

McIntosh apples.

McLean, Stuart. 2017. *Fictionalizing Anthropology: Encounters and Fabulations at the Edges of the Human*. Minneapolis: University of Minnesota Press.

Meanwhile.

Meiselas, Susan. 2015. "Reflecting on Photography and Human Rights." Lecture given at the University of Chicago, June 4.

Meloy, J. Reid, ed. 1998. *The Psychology of Stalking: Clinical and Forensic Perspectives*. San Diego: Academic Press.

Merport, Carmen. 2017. "Ripped from the Pages of *Life*: Sensation, Banality, and the Politics of Representation in Postwar American Art." Manuscript in preparation.

Milman, Oliver. 2016. "Piranhas with Human-like Teeth in Michigan Fuel Concern over Invasive Fish." *The Guardian*, August 16. https://www.theguardian.com/us-news/2016/aug/16/piranhas-human-like-teeth-michigan-invasive-tropical-fish?CMP=Share_iOSApp_Other.

Mitchell, Joni. 1974. "The Same Situation." On *Court and Spark*. Crazy Crow Music; Elektra/Asylum Records, 7E-1001, 33 1/3 RPM.

Mitchell, W. J. T. 1994. *Picture Theory*. Chicago: University of Chicago Press.

Mitchell, W. J. T. Forthcoming. *Seeing Madness: Up Close and from Afar*. Chicago: University of Chicago Press.

Moten, Fred. 2008a. "The Case of Blackness." *Criticism* 50 (2): 177–218.

Moten, Fred. 2008b. "Fugitivity Is Immanent to the Thing but Is Manifest Transversally." In *Hughson's Tavern*, 57. Providence, RI: Leon Works.

Moten, Fred. 2013. "Blackness and Nothingness (Mysticism in the Flesh)." *South Atlantic Quarterly* 112 (4): 737–80.

Muecke, Stephen. 2008. *Joe in the Andamans and Other Fictocritical Stories*. Sydney: Local Consumption.

Muecke, Stephen. 2016. *The Mother's Day Protest and Other Fictocritical Essays*. London: Rowman and Littlefield International.

Mullen, Harryette. 2002. *Sleeping with the Dictionary*. Berkeley: University of California Press.

Muñoz, José Esteban. 2009. *Cruising Utopia: The Then and There of Queer Futurity*. New York: New York University Press.

Nersessian, Anahid, and Jonathan Kramnick. 2017. "Form and Explanation." *Critical Inquiry* 43 (3): 650–69.

Ngai, Sianne. 2015. *Our Aesthetic Categories: Zany, Cute, Interesting*. Cambridge, MA: Harvard University Press.

Occupy.

Ogden, Thomas. 1997. "Reverie and Metaphor: Some Thoughts on How I Work as a Psychoanalyst." *International Journal of Psychoanalysis* 78 (4): 719–32.

O'Hara, Frank. (1960) 1995. "Having a Coke with You." In *The Collected Poems of Frank O'Hara*, edited by Donald Allen, 360. Berkeley: University of California Press.

One word changes the tone.

On the outs: wearing out; giving out; getting out; handing out; following out; going out; measuring out; seeking out; spinning out; feeling out; beating the shit out of; turned out; tricked out; checked out.

Ordinary registers—skittish, speculative, sedimenting, funny, overworked, saturated, with or without traction.

Osnos, Evan. 2017. "Doomsday Prep for the Super Rich." *New Yorker*, January 30.

Pandian, Anand, and Stuart McLean, eds. 2017. *Crumpled Paper Boat: Experiments in Ethnographic Writing*. Durham, NC: Duke University Press.

Parrish, Maxfield (painter).

Peanuts (the "wah wah" teacher voice). 1967. Originating in *You're in Love, Charlie Brown*, 30 min. Directed by Bill Melendez. Written by Charles Schulz. First aired June 12, on CBS.

Pencil and paper.

Perec, Georges. (1974) 2008. *Species of Spaces and Other Pieces*. Edited and translated by John Sturrock. London: Penguin Books.

Pine, Jason. 2012. *The Art of Making Do in Naples*. Minneapolis: University of Minnesota Press.

Pine, Jason. 2016. "Last Chance Incorporated." *Cultural Anthropology* 31 (2): 297–318. https://doi.org/10.14506/ca31.2.07.

Pita bread.

Poe, Edgar Allan. 1846. "Cask of Amontillado." http://xroads.virginia.edu /~hyper/poe/cask.html.

Posmentier, Sonya. 2017. *Cultivation and Catastrophe: The Lyric Ecology of Modern Black Literature*. Baltimore, MD: Johns Hopkins University Press.

Postone, Moishe. 2004. "Critique and Historical Transformation." *Historical Materialism* 12 (3): 53–72.

Preppers.

Pressure points.

Prince. 1988. "Anna Stesia." On *Lovesexy*. Paisley Park 25720–1, 33 1/3 RPM.

Prouty, Olive Higgins. 1941. *Now, Voyager*. New York: Houghton Mifflin.

Puar, Jasbir, ed. 2012. "Precarity Talk: A Virtual Roundtable with Lauren Berlant, Judith Butler, Bojana Cvejić, Isabell Lorey, Jasbir Puar, and Ana Vujanović." *TDR: The Drama Review* 56 (4): 163–77.

Puck.

Quick, Andrew. 1998. "Time and the Event." *Cultural Values* 2 (2–3): 223–42.

Quotidian ambitions.

Raffles, Hugh. 2002. "Intimate Knowledge." *International Social Science Journal* 54 (173): 325–35.

Raffles, Hugh. 2011. *Insectopedia*. New York: Vintage.

Raffles, Hugh. 2012. "TWENTY-FIVE YEARS IS A LONG TIME." *Cultural Anthropology* 27 (3): 526–34.

Rancière, Jacques. 2011. "The Thinking of Dissensus: Politics and Aesthetics." In *Reading Rancière: Critical Dissensus*, edited by Paul Bowman and Richard Stamp, 1–17. London: Continuum.

Ray, Nicholas (director). 1956. *Bigger Than Life*. Criterion Collection, 2010, DVD.

Receptivity. *See* encounter; spark. *See also* things that are tiring.

Red Bull.

Regan, Matthias. Co-ranter, Feel Tank Chicago, 2017.

Regan, Matthias, and Brian Holmes. 2016. *Watersheds*. Digital map that includes poems from *Police State*. http://midwestcompass.org /watersheds/map.html.

Reinhardt, Ad (painter).

Robinson, Roxana. 2009. *Cost*. New York: Picador.

Rose, Jacqueline. 1989. "Where Does the Misery Come From? Psychoanalysis, Feminism, and the Event." In *Feminism and Psychoanalysis*, edited by Richard Feldstein and Judith Roof, 25–39. Ithaca, NY: Cornell University Press.

Scantron.

Scappetone, Jennifer. 2016. *The Republic of Exit 43: Outtakes and Scores from an Archaeology and Pop-Up Opera of the Corporate Dump*. Berkeley, CA: Atelos.

Scott-Heron, Gil. 1970. "Comment #1." On *Small Talk at 125th and Lenox*. New York: Flying Dutchman Records, OST013LP, 33 1/3 RPM.

Search engines.

Search Party.

Sedgwick, Eve Kosofsky. 1990. *Epistemology of the Closet.* Berkeley: University of California Press.

Sedgwick, Eve Kosofsky. 1993. "White Glasses." In *Tendencies,* 252–66. Durham, NC: Duke University Press.

Sedgwick, Eve Kosofsky. 1997. "Paranoid Reading and Reparative Reading: Or, You're So Paranoid, You Probably Think This Introduction Is about You." In *Novel Gazing: Queer Readings in Fiction,* edited by Eve Kosofsky Sedgwick, 1–37. Durham, NC: Duke University Press.

Seigworth, Gregory. 1998. "Houses in Motion." *Antithesis* 9:9–24.

Seigworth, Gregory, and Matthew Tiessen. 2012. "Mobile Affects, Open Secrets, and Global Illiquidity: Pockets, Pools, and Plasma." *Theory, Culture, and Society* 29 (6): 47–77.

Self-defeating DIY house-for-sale photographs: posted online, passionately captioned, too much, too late, too little. *See* "all wrong."

Serial immersion.

Serres, Michel. 1997. *Genesis.* Translated by Geneviève James and James Nielson. Ann Arbor: University of Michigan Press.

Shaviro, Steven. 2016. *Discognition.* London: Repeater Press.

Simon, David Carroll. 2017. "The Anatomy of Schadenfreude; or, Montaigne's Laughter." *Critical Inquiry* 43 (2): 250–80.

Simon, David Carroll. 2018. *Light without Heat: The Observational Mood from Bacon to Milton.* Ithaca, NY: Cornell University Press.

Sister talk over decades.

Solomon, Andrew. 1998. "Anatomy of Melancholy." *New Yorker,* January 12. http://www.newyorker.com/magazine/1998/01/12/anatomy-of -melancholy.

Some hooks: the precisions of a walk, a look, a predation, a pause, a stuttering, the history of sugar.

Spahr, Juliana. 2005. *The Connection of Everything with Lungs: Poems.* Berkeley: University of California Press.

Spahr, Juliana. 2011. *Well Then There Now.* Boston: Black Sparrow Press.

Spillers, Hortense. 2003. *Black, White, and in Color: Essays on American Literature and Culture.* Chicago: University of Chicago Press.

Star Trek. Originated by Gene Roddenberry. NBC, 1966–1969.

Stengers, Isabella, Brian Massumi, and Erin Manning. 2009. "History through the Middle: Between Macro and Mesopolitics—an Interview with Isabella Stengers." *Inflexions: A Journal of Research Creation*, no. 3. http://www.inflexions.org/n3_stengershtml.html.

Stern, Lesley. 2001. *The Smoking Book*. Chicago: University of Chicago Press.

Stern, Lesley, and Kathleen Stewart. 2016. "Companion Pieces Written Through a Drift." In *Sensitive Objects*, edited by Jonas Frykman and Maja Povrzanović Frykman, 257–74. Lund, Sweden: Nordic Academic Press.

Stevens, Wallace. (1957) 1990. *Opus Posthumous*. Edited by Milton Bates. New York: Vintage.

Stewart, Kathleen. 2007. *Ordinary Affects*. Durham, NC: Duke University Press.

Stillinger, Thomas C. 1991. Personal communication.

Stockton, Kathryn Bond. 2009. *The Queer Child: Or Growing Sideways in the Twentieth Century*. Durham, NC: Duke University Press.

Story problems.

Strike Debt!

Suicidiation.

Sunset magazine.

Surfaces: suspension, proximity, patina, pattern.

Surprise: being tripwired, being ready, being in the middle, being off base, being all ears.

Sutherland, Keston. 2009. *Stress Position*. London: Barque Press.

Taussig, Michael. 1992. *The Nervous System*. London: Routledge.

Taussig, Michael. 2011. *I Swear I Saw This*. Chicago. University of Chicago Press.

Taylor, Christopher. 2014. Red Pants (personal wardrobe).

Taylor, Christopher. 2015. "Thoughts and Prayers and the Terror of Politics." *Of C. L. R. James*, December 3. http://clrjames.blogspot.com/2015/12/thoughts-and-prayers-and-terror-of.html.

Temple, Shirley (a person and a cocktail).

Text message jams when a comment pinged on threads that took off.

The body: a contact sheet with a nervous system, mouths opening and closing.

The built environment.

The ethnographic ground.

The historical present.

The nap of corduroy.

The Voice.

Things people say about clichés.

Things that are spoken, but not loudly.

Things we noticed that other people were noticing too (or not quite).

Things we said to each other: "That's so funny!" "I don't know what you mean." "Who wrote that?"

Thought. *See* afterthought. *See also* pragmatics; composition; comfort food; imperatives (think about this, see that, remember that, clean that up).

Tipping points into expressivity, things toppling over.

Tomatoes.

Townies.

Tremblay, Jean-Thomas. 2018. "We Don't Breathe Alone: Forms of Encounter in Anglophone North America Since the 1970s." Ph.D. dissertation. University of Chicago.

Trump, Donald. https://en.wikiquote.org/wiki/Donald_Trump.

Trusting. *See* testing.

Try It Out Bags.

Tsing, Anna Lowenhaupt. 2005. *Friction: An Ethnography of Global Connection.* Princeton, NJ: Princeton University Press.

"Under Pressure" 1982. Written and recorded by Queen with David Bowie. On *Hot Space*. Island Records 277 175 8, 2011, compact disc.

Voice Dream.

Wainwright, Loudon, III. 1973. "The Swimming Song." On *Attempted Mustache*. Columbia Records KC 32710, 33 1/3 RPM.

Wallace, David Foster. (2005) 2009. *This Is Water: Some Thoughts, Delivered on a Significant Occasion, about Living a Compassionate Life.* New York: Little, Brown.

Warner, Michael. 1991. "The Mass Public and the Mass Subject." In *Habermas and the Public Sphere*, edited by Craig Calhoun, 377–401. Cambridge, MA: MIT Press.

Ways of being up for it.

Weak links (people, machines, systems, now).

Weeks, Kathi. 2011. *The Problem with Work: Feminism, Marxism, Antiwork Politics, and Postwork Imaginaries.* Durham, NC: Duke University Press.

Welty, Eudora. 1994. "Petrified Man." In *The Collected Stories of Eudora Welty*, 17–28. Boston: Houghton Mifflin Harcourt.

When being long-winded adds something (the whole week's shakes or telling the whole story even though you need only a detail).

When being short-tempered adds something.

Whitehead, Colson. 1999. *The Intuitionist*. New York: Anchor Books.

Wilderson, Frank, with Jared Ball, Todd Steven Burroughs, and Dr. Hate. 2014. "'We're trying to destroy the world': Anti-Blackness & Police Violence After Ferguson. An Interview with Frank B. Wilderson, III." Ill Will Editions, November. http://ill-will-editions.tumblr.com /post/103584583009/were-trying-to-destroy-the-world.

Williams, Patricia. 2005. "Salt in the Wound: Why Is *The New York Times Magazine* Floating an Unsubstantiated Theory of Genetic Determinism?" *The Nation*, June 6. https://www.thenation.com/article/salt-wound/.

Winnicott, D. W. (1971) 1982. *Playing and Reality*. New York: Basic Books.

Wiseman, Frederick (director). 2001. *Domestic Violence*. 16 mm film, 196 min. Cambridge, MA: Zipporah Films.

Wittgenstein, Ludwig. 2009. *Philosophical Investigations*. Translated and edited by P. M. S. Hacker and Joachim Schulte. Rev. 4th ed. Oxford: Wiley-Blackwell.

Worlds—provisional movements, dreams of cohesion, sensations of being in something heady but real, a promise charged with retractability, what appears when a rhythm is interrupted. Wrecked, try to write back into form or sense.

X and its effects. *See* surrealism and work.

YMCA.

Yummly.

Zerilli, Linda M. G. 2005. *Feminism and the Abyss of Freedom*. Chicago: University of Chicago Press.

Žižek, Slavoj. 2004. "Passion in the Era of Decaffeinated Belief." *Lacanian Ink*, no. 5. http://www.lacan.com/passionf.htm.

Žižek, Slavoj. 2014. *Žižek's Jokes: (Did You Hear the One about Hegel and Negation?)*. Edited by Audun Mortensen. Cambridge, MA: MIT Press.